THE ULTIMATE SANDWICH COOKBOOK

Elevate Your Sandwich Game with Over 100 Mouthwatering Recipes Featuring Fresh Ingredients, Classic Combinations, and Unique Twists

FERDINAND WARD

Copyright Material ©2023

All Rights Reserved

Without the proper written consent of the publisher and copyright owner, this book cannot be used or distributed in any way, shape, or form, except for brief quotations used in a review. This book should not be considered a substitute for medical, legal, or other professional advice.

TABLE OF CONTENTS

TABLE OF CONTENTS 3
INTRODUCTION 7
   1. Curried Shrimp-Stacked Tomatoes 8
   2. Turkey and Avocado Sandwich 10
   3. Veggie and Hummus Sandwich 12
   4. Tuna Salad Sandwich 14
   5. Grilled Cheddar Sandwich 16
   6. BLT Sandwich 18
   7. Coconut Bacon Reuben Sandwich 20
   8. Grilled Cheese And Tomato 22
   9. Lox, Tomato, Red Onion, And Capers 24
   10. Blt Club 26
   11. Mock Tuna Salad 28
   12. Cinnamon-Apple Open-Faced Sandwich 30
   13. Pumpkin cheese sandwiches 32
   14. Barbecued duck sandwich 34
   15. Pork Loin Sandwich 36
   16. Paneer Bhurji Sandwich 39
   17. Pimento Cheese and Tomato Sandwich 41
   18. Hassel back Tomato Clubs 44
   19. Fried Green Napoleons with Coleslaw 46
   20. Baked Eggplant Sandwiches 48
   21. Apple, Ham, and Cheese Sandwiches 51
   22. Cucumber Subs 53
   23. Breadless Italian Sub Sandwich 55
   24. Turkey Sliders with Sweet Potato 58

25. White castle hamburger sliders 60

26. Cheeseburger Sliders 62

27. Tempeh Reuben Sandwiches 64

28. Tastes like Tuna Salad Sandwiches 66

29. Sloppy Bulgur Sandwiches 68

30. Garden Patch Sandwiches on Bread 70

31. Fruit-And-Nut Sandwiches 72

32. Chicken and Waffles Grilled Cheese 74

33. Grilled Ham and Cheese Waffle Sandwiches 76

34. Pepperoni, Provolone and Pecorino Pita! 78

35. Grilled Cheddar, Chutney and Sausage 80

36. Curried Tofu "Egg Salad" Pitas 82

37. Prosciutto and Taleggio with Figs on Mesclun 84

38. Fontina with Arugula, Mizuna and Pears 86

39. Chèvre Sandwiches in Salad 88

40. Sizzled Halloumi Sandwiches with Lime 91

41. Truffled Toast and Arugula Salad 93

42. Ham, Cheese and Pineapple 95

43. Ricotta Granola Crumble Grilled Cheese 97

44. Lasagna Grilled Cheese 99

45. Italian Classic Grilled Cheese 101

46. Mediterranean Meatball Grilled Cheese 103

47. Spinach Pesto and Avocado Grilled Cheese 105

48. Strawberry Basil Prosciutto Grilled Cheese 107

49. Ricotta Butter and Jam Grilled Cheese 109

50. Buffalo Chicken Grilled Cheese 111

51. Veggie Pizza Grilled Cheese 113

52. Cheddar and Sourdough Grilled cheese 115

53. Grilled cheese sandwich 117

54. Spinach and Dill Havarti Sandwich 119

55. Grilled Jack on Rye with Mustard 121

56. Radicchio and Roquefort on Pain au Levain 123

57. Garlic Grilled Cheese on Rye 125

58. British Melted Cheese and Pickle 127

59. **Fresh Mozzarella, Prosciutto and Fig Jam** 129

60. **Rare Roast Beef with Blue Cheese** 131

61. Red Leicester with Onion 133

62. Spinach and Dill Havarti on Bread 135

63. Open-Faced Grilled Cheddar and Dill Pickle 137

64. Harry's Bar Special 139

65. Casse Croûte of Blue Cheese and Gruyère 141

66. Crisp Truffled Comté with Black Chanterelles 143

67. Goat Cheese Toasts with Spices 146

68. Roquefort Sandwiches and Beet Marmalade 148

69. Bocadillo from the Island of Ibiza 151

70. Club Grilled Sandwich 154

71. Welsh Rarebit with Poached Egg 157

72. A Hot Muffaletta 160

73. Cuban Sandwich 162

74. Parisian Grilled Cheese 165

75. Bocadillo from the Island of Ibiza 167

76. Tomato and Mahon Cheese on Olive Bread 169

77. Emmentaler and Pear Sandwich 171

78. Grilled Pumpernickel and Gouda 173

79. Smoked Turkey, Taleggio and Gorgonzola 175

80. Melted Jarlsberg on Sourdough 177

81. Torta of Chicken, Queso Fresco, and Gouda 179

82. Panini of Eggplant Parmigiana 182

83. Grilled Eggplant and Chaumes 185
84. Mushrooms and Melted Cheese on Pain au Levain 188
85. Sicilian Sizzled Cheese with Capers and Artichokes 191
86. Scaloppine and Pesto sandwich 193
87. Mozzarella, Basil Piadine 196
88. Quesadillas on Pumpkin Tortillas 198
89. Grilled Sheep Cheese Quesadillas 201
90. Toast with Strawberries and Cream Cheese 203
91. Bread Pudding Sandwiches 206
92. Grain and cheese burger 209
93. Black angus burger with cheddar cheese 211
94. Grilled American cheese and tomato sandwich 213
95. Grilled apple and cheese 215
96. Grilled blue cheese sandwiches with walnuts 217
97. Grilled cheddar cheese and ham sandwiches 219
98. Party Grilled cheese and bacon 221
99. Grilled cheese gobblers 223
100. Grilled cheese in French toast 225

CONCLUSION 227

INTRODUCTION

Are you tired of the same old sandwich combinations? Do you want to impress your friends and family with creative and delicious sandwiches? Look no further than The Ultimate Sandwich Cookbook!

This cookbook features over 100 recipes for sandwiches that will satisfy any craving, from classic combinations like BLTs and grilled cheese, to unique twists like a banh mi-inspired sub or a grilled veggie and hummus wrap. Each recipe features fresh ingredients and easy-to-follow instructions that will have you creating amazing sandwiches in no time.

But it's not just about the fillings – this cookbook also includes recipes for homemade breads, rolls, and spreads that will take your sandwiches to the next level. Whether you're looking for a quick lunch, a picnic snack, or a crowd-pleasing party platter, The Ultimate Sandwich Cookbook has you covered.

So why settle for boring sandwiches when you can elevate your sandwich game with this cookbook? With recipes for every occasion and taste, you'll never run out of delicious sandwich ideas.

sandwich cookbook, sandwich recipes, creative sandwiches, delicious sandwiches, fresh ingredients, unique twists, classic combinations, homemade bread, spreads, lunch, picnic, party platter.

1. **Curried Shrimp-Stacked Tomatoes**

Makes 4 servings

INGREDIENTS
- 4 large heirloom tomatoes
- 6 tablespoons reduced-fat mayonnaise
- 1 teaspoon curry powder
- 1/4 teaspoon salt
- 1/4 teaspoon ground ginger
- 3/4 pound peeled and deveined cooked shrimp
- 1 celery rib, chopped
- 1/2 cup finely chopped cucumber
- 1 small navel orange, peeled and finely chopped
- 2 green onions, thinly sliced

INSTRUCTIONS
a) Trim and cut each tomato into three thick slices; drain on paper towels.
b) In a large bowl, mix mayonnaise and seasonings; stir in remaining ingredients. For each serving, stack three slices tomatoes, layering with shrimp mixture.

2. Turkey and Avocado Sandwich

INGREDIENTS
- 2 slices whole wheat bread
- 2-3 slices turkey breast
- 1/4 avocado, sliced
- 1 slice cheddar cheese
- 1 tablespoon mayonnaise
- 1 teaspoon Dijon mustard
- Lettuce and tomato, optional

INSTRUCTIONS:
a) Toast the bread slices until lightly golden.
b) Spread mayonnaise and Dijon mustard on one side of each bread slice.
c) Layer the turkey, avocado, cheese, lettuce, and tomato between the bread slices.
d) Cut the sandwich in half and serve.

3. Veggie and Hummus Sandwich

INGREDIENTS
- 2 slices whole grain bread
- 2 tablespoons hummus
- 1/4 cup shredded carrots
- 1/4 cup sliced cucumber
- 1/4 cup sliced red bell pepper
- 1 slice cheddar cheese
- Salt and pepper to taste

INSTRUCTIONS:
a) Toast the bread slices until lightly golden.
b) Spread hummus on one side of each bread slice.
c) Layer the shredded carrots, sliced cucumber, red bell pepper, and cheddar cheese between the bread slices.
d) Season with salt and pepper to taste.
e) Cut the sandwich in half and serve.

4. Tuna Salad Sandwich

INGREDIENTS
- 2 slices white bread
- 1 can tuna, drained
- 1/4 cup diced celery
- 1/4 cup diced onion
- 2 tablespoons mayonnaise
- 1 teaspoon Dijon mustard
- Salt and pepper to taste
- Lettuce and tomato, optional

INSTRUCTIONS:

a) Toast the bread slices until lightly golden.
b) In a bowl, mix together the tuna, celery, onion, mayonnaise, Dijon mustard, salt, and pepper.
c) Layer the tuna salad, lettuce, and tomato between the bread slices.
d) Cut the sandwich in half and serve.

5. Grilled Cheddar Sandwich

INGREDIENTS
- 2 slices sourdough bread
- 2 slices cheddar cheese
- 2 tablespoons butter

INSTRUCTIONS:
a) Heat a non-stick skillet over medium heat.
b) Butter one side of each bread slice.
c) Place one slice of bread, butter-side down, onto the skillet.
d) Top with the cheddar cheese slices and the second bread slice, butter-side up.
e) Cook until the bread is golden brown and the cheese is melted, about 2-3 minutes per side.
f) Cut the sandwich in half and serve.

6. BLT Sandwich

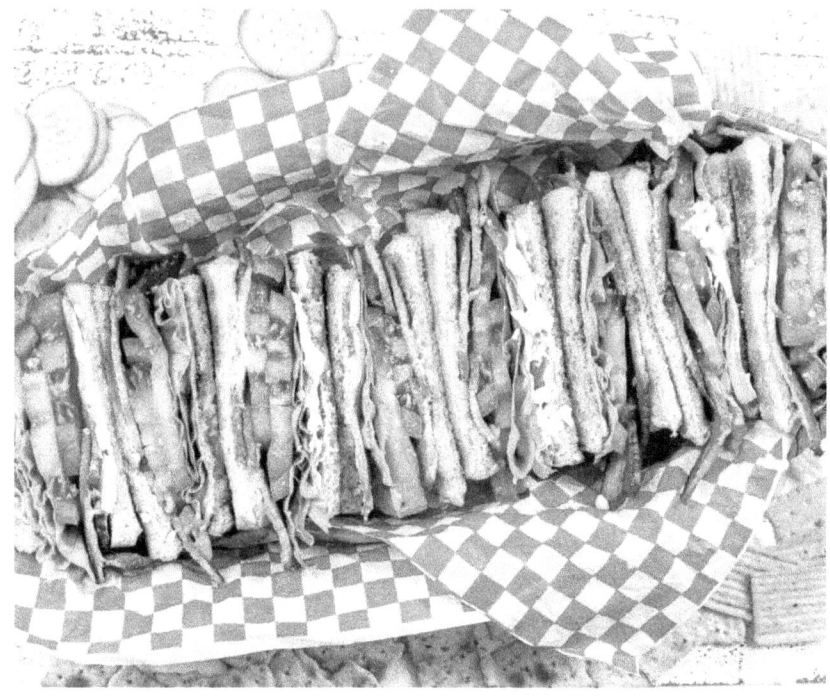

INGREDIENTS
- 2 slices white bread
- 3 strips bacon, cooked
- 1/4 avocado, sliced
- 2 slices tomato
- 1 tablespoon mayonnaise
- Lettuce

INSTRUCTIONS:
a) Toast the bread slices until lightly golden.
b) Spread mayonnaise on one side of each bread slice.
c) Layer the bacon, avocado, tomato, and lettuce between the bread slices.
d) Cut the sandwich in half and serve.

7. Coconut Bacon Reuben Sandwich

MAKES 4 SANDWICHES

INGREDIENTS
- 1 recipe Rye Flatbread
- 1 recipe of your favorite Cheese
- 1 recipe Coconut Bacon or Eggplant Bacon
- 1 recipe Thousand Island Dressing
- 1 cup of your favorite sauerkraut

INSTRUCTIONS:
a) Place a slice of Rye Flatbread on each of four serving dishes.
b) Spread with a layer of Cheese.
c) Top with slices of Coconut Bacon and drizzle with Thousand Island Dressing.
d) Top with sauerkraut and a second piece of flatbread, and serve immediately.

8. Grilled Cheese And Tomato

MAKES 4 SERVINGS

INGREDIENTS
- 8 slices of Zucchini Bread   or Sunflower Bread
- 1 recipe of your favorite Cheese Sauce
- 1 tomato, seeded and sliced thickly

INSTRUCTIONS:
a) Place a slice of bread on each of four serving dishes. Spread each with about ¼ cup of Cheese.
b) Top with a slice of tomato and a second slice of bread.
c) Serve immediately.

9. Lox, Tomato, Red Onion, And Capers

MAKES 4 SANDWICHES

INGREDIENTS
- 8 slices of your favorite bread
- ¼ cup Aioli Mayonnaise
- 1 tomato, seeded and sliced
- 1 cup sliced mango or Thai young coconut meat
- ½ cup arugula
- ¼ cup sliced red onion
- ¼ cup drained capers

INSTRUCTIONS:
a) Place a slice of bread on each of four serving dishes. Spread each portion with 2 tablespoons of Aioli Mayonnaise.
b) Top with the tomato slices, then the mango, arugula, onion, and capers, and finally the remaining bread.
c) Will keep for several hours.

10. Blt Club

MAKES 4 SERVINGS

INGREDIENTS
- 12 slices of Zucchini Bread or Sunflower Bread
- 1 recipe Aioli Mayonnaise
- 8 leaves iceberg lettuce
- 1 tomato, seeded and sliced
- 1 ripe avocado, pitted and sliced
- 1 recipe Coconut Bacon

INSTRUCTIONS:

a) Place a slice of bread on each of four serving dishes and spread with a couple of tablespoons of Mayonnaise. Top each portion with a lettuce leaf, then a slice of tomato, some avocado, and then another slice of bread. Spread that slice with additional Mayonnaise, and top with slices of Coconut Bacon, lettuce, and tomato. Spread a couple of tablespoons of Mayonnaise on one side of the remaining slices of bread, and place Mayonnaise side down atop your sandwiches.

b) The assembled sandwich will keep for a few hours.

11. Mock Tuna Salad

MAKES 4 SERVINGS

INGREDIENTS
- 1 recipe Aioli Mayonnaise
- 3 cups carrot pulp
- 1 cup chopped celery
- ¼ cup chopped yellow onion
- 1 recipe of your favorite bread

INSTRUCTIONS:
a) Place the Aioli Mayonnaise, carrot pulp, celery, and onion in a mixing bowl. Mix well.
b) Assemble your sandwiches by spreading one-quarter of the mixture between two slices of bread. Top with sliced tomato and iceberg lettuce. Repeat to make the remaining sandwiches.
c) The assembled sandwiches will keep for a couple of hours. Mock Tuna Salad will keep for 2 days when stored separately in the fridge.

12. Cinnamon-Apple Open-Faced Sandwich

MAKES 4 SERVINGS

INGREDIENTS
- 1 recipe Miso Butter , Vanilla Butter , Lavender Butter, or Chocolate Butter
- 1 apple, cored and sliced
- ¼ cup agave syrup
- 1 teaspoon ground cinnamon

INSTRUCTIONS:
a) Place a slice of bread on each of four serving dishes. Spread each slice with your choice of butter.
b) Top with sliced apples, drizzle with agave syrup, and sprinkle cinnamon on top.
c) Will keep for a day.

13. Pumpkin cheese sandwiches

Makes: 16 servings

INGREDIENTS:
- 16 slices White or whole wheat bread
- 8 slices White cheese such as Jack
- 4 large Pitted black olives
- 8 slices Cheddar cheese
- 1 can Chopped black olives
- 4 large Pitted green olives
- 12 Pimento slices

INSTRUCTIONS:
a)   Press ghost cookie cutter into 1 bread slice. Tear off and discard excess bread around the cutter; set a ghost-shaped piece of bread aside. Repeat with 7 more bread slices.
b)   Using a pumpkin cookie cutter, cut the remaining bread into pumpkin shapes in the same manner.
c)   Toast "ghosts" and "pumpkins" under the broiler until golden brown, about 1 minute. Turnover and repeat on another side.
d)   Remove bread from oven and set aside. Use a ghost cookie cutter to cut 8 ghost shapes from white cheese slices. With a small sharp knife, cut two eye holes in each white cheese slice. Make sure the "eyes" are large enough to stay open when the cheese melts. Slice black olives in half lengthwise.
e)   Place on ghost bread slices where the ghosts' eyes will go. Place 1 ghost-shaped slice of white cheese on 1 ghost bread slice with eye holes over olives. Repeat with remaining ghost bread and white cheese.
f)   Use a pumpkin cookie cutter to cut 8 pumpkin shapes from orange cheese slices. Cut 2 eye holes and mouth into each cheese slice. Cover the surface of pumpkin bread slices with chopped black olives. Slice green olives in half lengthwise.
g)   Place one green olive slice on the stem and trim to fit. Place orange cheese on top of bread and olives. Put pimento slices in.
h)   Place all sandwiches on a baking sheet and set under the broiler until cheese is slightly melted 1 to 2 minutes.

14. Barbecued duck sandwich

Makes: 2 servings

INGREDIENTS:
- 1 duck meat from 1 whole roasted duck
- 1 cup homemade or prepared barbecue sauce
- 1 tablespoon thinly-sliced green onions
- 2 onion rolls
- 1 bag potato chips; optional

Thinly slice duck into bite-size strips. In a small saucepan combine duck, barbecue sauce and green onions and heat through. Slice open rolls and toast them. Fill each roll with a generous portion of duck mixture. Serve garnished with some potato chips.

15. Pork Loin Sandwich

INGREDIENTS:
- 2–4 slices roast pork with crackling
- 4 tablespoons—sweet–sour red cabbage
- 3 tablespoons good-quality mayonnaise
- 1 tablespoon strong, coarse mustard
- 2 pickles, sliced
- 1 lady apple
- Some red onion rings (optional)

SOUR–SWEET RED CABBAGE
- 1 medium red cabbage
- 1/2 bottle red wine
- Spices: clove, bay leaves, cinnamon stick, pepper, star anise
- 2 onions
- Salt
- 3 tablespoons duck or goose fat
- 2 cups balsamic or cider vinegar
- 2 tablespoons cane sugar, depending on the sweetness of wine and vinegar

INSTRUCTIONS:
a) Warm up pork loin and red cabbage if necessary.
b) Stir mayonnaise with mustard and spread on bread slices.
c) Place red cabbage, meat, sliced gherkins, sliced apple, and onion rings in layers on one slice of bread and close with the other slice to make a sandwich.
d) Boil red wine with dried spices for 5 minutes and leave to infuse for 15 minutes.
e) Remove stem from cabbage head if there is one and shred it. Peel and chop onion.
f) Sauté red cabbage and onion in goose fat in large thick-bottomed pan.
g) Pour red wine through a sieve to remove the spices into pan and add salt.

h) Leave to simmer for at least one hour—several hours' cooking will give a soft and wonderfully tasty cabbage.
i) Season red cabbage with vinegar and sugar.

16. Paneer Bhurji Sandwich

Makes: 2 Servings

INGREDIENTS:
- ½ teaspoon Green Chilies, chopped
- 1½ tablespoons Fresh Coriander, chopped
- 4 Bread Slices
- ½ cup Cottage Cheese
- 2 tablespoons Tomatoes
- ¼ teaspoon Pepper Powder
- A pinch of Turmeric Powder
- ¼ teaspoon Cumin Seeds
- Salt
- 1½ teaspoons Clarified Butter

INSTRUCTIONS
a) In a pan, heat ghee or oil and add cumin seeds.
b) When the seeds begin to crackle, add the green chilies and stir.
c) Stir in the chopped tomato for a few seconds, or until it softens.
d) Mix in the turmeric and paneer.
e) Stir in the pepper powder, and salt, and stir for a few seconds.
f) Mix in the chopped coriander in the pan.
g) Spread butter on one side of each loaf of bread.
h) Place a slice on the grill and spread half of the paneer stuffing over it.
i) Cover with another piece of bread, butter side up, and grill until golden.
j) Remove from the grill and cut into two pieces.

17. Pimento Cheese and Tomato Sandwich

Makes: 8 TO 12 SERVINGS

INGREDIENTS:
FOR THE CHEESE SPREAD:
- ½ cup mayonnaise
- 4 ounces cream cheese
- 3 cups shredded sharp cheddar cheese
- 1 (4-ounce) jar of diced pimentos, drained
- 1 tablespoon minced yellow onion
- 1 teaspoon minced garlic
- 1 teaspoon Worcestershire sauce
- ½ teaspoon ground black pepper

FOR THE TOMATOES:
- 1 cup self-rising flour
- 1 cup Polenta
- ½ teaspoon kosher salt
- ½ teaspoon ground black pepper
- 2 eggs
- ½ cup buttermilk
- 4 large green tomatoes, sliced ½ inch thick
- 2 cups vegetable oil, for deep-frying
- 2 loaves French bread, sliced in half lengthwise

INSTRUCTIONS:
a) In a large bowl, combine the mayonnaise and cream cheese, and mix until well combined. Add the cheddar cheese, pimentos, onion, garlic, Worcestershire sauce, and black pepper. Mix until well incorporated, cover the bowl, and refrigerate for a minimum of 6 hours.

b) In a medium mixing bowl, combine the self-rising flour, Polenta, salt, and black pepper. Mix until well incorporated and set aside.

c) In another medium mixing bowl, combine the eggs and buttermilk, and mix well.

d) Pat the sliced tomatoes dry with paper towels. Dip the tomatoes into the egg mixture, then into the flour mixture. Let the tomatoes sit for 5 minutes.

e) In a large skillet over medium heat, pour the vegetable oil until it's 2 to 3 inches deep. Add the tomatoes and deep-fry until nice and golden, 3 to 4 minutes.

f) Slather the pimento cheese on the bottom half of the French bread, then top off with the fried tomatoes and the top half of the French bread. Cut into individual sandwiches and serve.

18. Hassel back Tomato Clubs

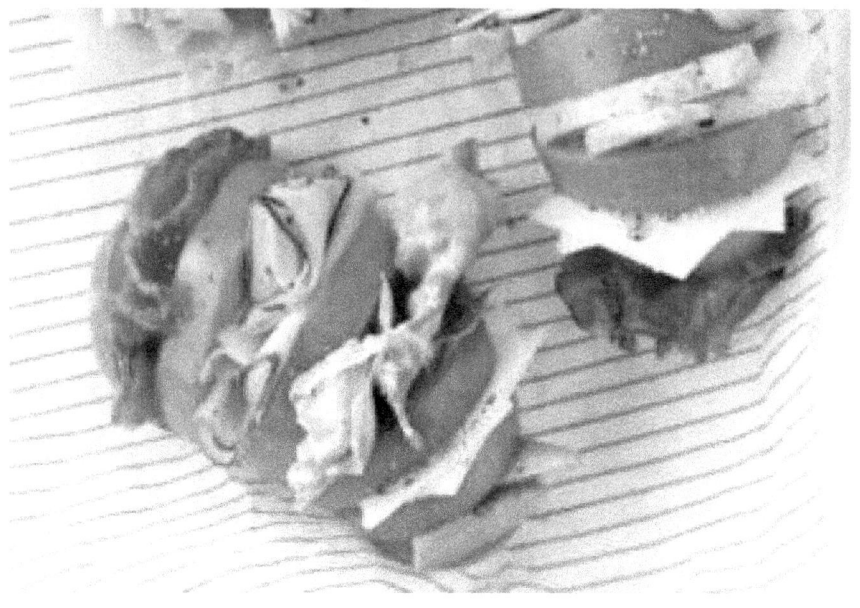

Makes 2 servings

INGREDIENTS
- 4 plum tomatoes
- 2 slices Swiss cheese, quartered
- 4 cooked bacon strips, halved
- 4 slices deli turkey
- 4 Bibb lettuce leaves
- 1/2 medium ripe avocado, peeled and cut into 8 slices
- Cracked pepper

INSTRUCTIONS

a) Cut 4 crosswise slices in each tomato, leaving them intact at the bottom.
b) Fill each slice with cheese, bacon, turkey, lettuce and avocado. Sprinkle with pepper.

19. Fried Green Napoleons with Coleslaw

INGREDIENTS

- 1/3 cup mayonnaise
- 1/4 cup white vinegar
- 2 tablespoons sugar
- 1 teaspoon salt
- 1 teaspoon garlic powder
- 1/2 teaspoon pepper
- 1 package (14 ounces) three-color coleslaw mix
- 1/4 cup finely chopped onion
- 1 can (11 ounces) mandarin oranges, drained
- fried tomatoes:
- 1 large egg, lightly beaten
- Dash hot pepper sauce, or to taste
- 1/4 cup all-purpose flour
- 1 cup dry crumbs
- 2 medium green tomatoes, cut into 4 slices each
- Oil for frying
- 1/2 teaspoon salt
- 1/4 teaspoon pepper
- 1/2 cup refrigerated pimiento cheese
- 4 teaspoons pepper jelly

INSTRUCTIONS

a) Combine first six ingredients. Add coleslaw mix and onion. Add mandarin oranges; stir carefully.
b) In a shallow bowl, whisk egg and hot sauce. Place flour and crumbs in separate shallow bowls. Dip tomato slices in flour to coat both sides; shake off excess. Dip in egg mixture, then in crumbs, patting to help coating adhere.
c) In an electric skillet or deep fryer, heat oil to 350°. Fry tomato slices, a few at a time, until browned, 1-2 minutes on each side. Drain on paper towels. Sprinkle with salt and pepper.
d) To assemble napoleons, layer one tomato slice with 1 tablespoon pimiento cheese. Repeat layers. Top with 1 teaspoon pepper jelly. Repeat with remaining tomato slices. Serve over coleslaw.

20. Baked Eggplant Sandwiches

Servings: 4

INGREDIENTS
- 1 teaspoon olive oil
- 2 eggs
- ½ cup all-purpose flour, or more as needed
- salt and freshly ground black pepper to taste
- 1 pinch cayenne pepper, or more to taste
- 1 cup panko crumbs
- 8 slices of eggplant, cut 3/8 inch thick
- 2 slices provolone cheese, cut into quarters
- 12 thin slices salami
- 2 ⅔ tablespoons olive oil, divided
- 2 ⅔ tablespoons finely grated Parmigiano-Reggiano cheese, divided

INSTRUCTIONS

a) Preheat oven to 425 degrees F (220 degrees C). Line a baking sheet with aluminum foil.

b) Beat eggs in a small, shallow bowl. Mix flour, salt, black pepper, and cayenne pepper in a large shallow dish. Pour panko crumbs in another large shallow dish.

c) Top one slice of eggplant with 1/4 slice provolone cheese, 3 slices salami, and 1/4 slice provolone cheese. Place an equally-sized slice of eggplant on top. Repeat with remaining eggplant slices, cheese, and salami.

d) Gently press each eggplant sandwich into the seasoned flour to coat; shake off excess. Dip both sides of each sandwich into beaten egg, then press into panko crumbs. Place on the prepared baking sheet while you make the remaining eggplant sandwiches.

e) Drizzle 1 teaspoon olive oil in a circle about 3 inches in diameter onto the foil; place an eggplant sandwich onto the oiled area. Sprinkle about 1 teaspoon Parmigiano-Reggiano cheese over the sandwich. Repeat with remaining 3 sandwiches, drizzling an area on the foil with olive oil, placing a sandwich onto the oil, and topping with Parmesan cheese. Drizzle tops of each sandwich with 1 teaspoon olive oil.

f) Bake in the preheated oven for 10 minutes. Flip sandwiches and sprinkle 1 teaspoon Parmigiano-Reggiano cheese onto the top. Bake until browned and a paring knife inserts easily into the eggplant, 8 to 10 more minutes. Serve warm or at room temperature.

21. Apple, Ham, and Cheese Sandwiches

Servings: 2

INGREDIENTS
- apple
- Ham slices
- Colby Jack Slices
- Brown Mustard, Dijon style or condiment of choice

INSTRUCTIONS
a) Slice apples into rings.
b) Add Ham slices. Top with cheese slices.
c) Spread mustard on the top ring of the sandwich and place on top (condiment side down).

22. Cucumber Subs

SERVES 2

INGREDIENTS
- 2 cucumbers
- deli meat-turkey, ham, or other deli meat slices or shaved
- bacon (optional)
- green onions (optional)
- tomatoes (optional)
- any sandwich fillers (optional)
- laughing cow cheese or mayo or cream cheese or any other condiment

INSTRUCTIONS

a) Cut the cucumber length-wise, from tip to tip. Scoop out the inside of the cucumber to make room for your sandwich fillers. Add meat, veggies, and other sandwich makings to the inside of the cucumber.

b) Place one half of the cucumber on the other half. Enjoy!!

23. Breadless Italian Sub Sandwich

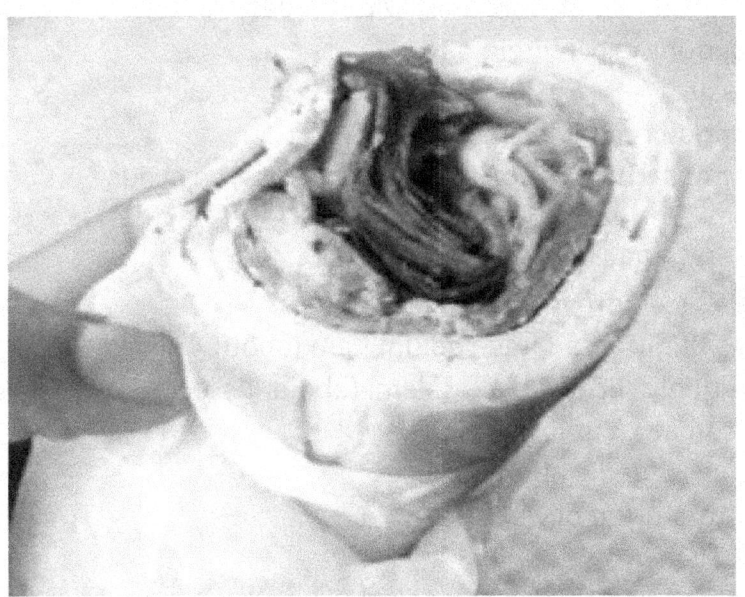

Yield: 4 sandwiches

INGREDIENTS
- 8 large Portobello mushrooms, wiped clean
- 2 tablespoons extra-virgin olive oil
- Kosher salt
- 1 tablespoon red wine vinegar
- 1 tablespoon finely chopped pepperoncini with seeds
- 1/2 teaspoon dried oregano
- Freshly ground black pepper
- 2 ounces sliced provolone (about 4 slices)
- 2 ounces thinly sliced low-sodium ham (about 4 slices)
- 1 ounce thinly sliced Genoa salami (about 4 slices)
- 1 small tomato, cut into 4 slices
- 1/2 cup shredded iceberg lettuce
- 4 pimento-stuffed olives

INSTRUCTIONS

a) Position an oven rack in the top third of the oven and preheat the oven broiler.

b) Remove the stems from the mushrooms and discard. Lay the mushroom caps gill-side-up and use a sharp knife to completely remove the gills (so that the caps will lie flat). Arrange the mushroom caps on a baking sheet, brush all over with 1 tablespoon of oil and sprinkle with 1/4 teaspoon salt. Broil until the caps are just tender, flipping halfway through, 4 to 5 minutes per side. Allow to cool completely.

c) Whisk together the vinegar, pepperoncini, oregano, remaining 1 tablespoon oil and a few grinds of black pepper in a small bowl.

d) Assemble the sandwiches: Arrange one mushroom cap, cut side-up, on a work surface. Fold 1 piece of provolone to fit on top of the cap and repeat with 1 slice each of ham and salami.

e) Top with 1 slice of tomato and about 2 tablespoons of lettuce. Drizzle with some of the pepperoncini vinaigrette. Sandwich with another mushroom cap and secure with a toothpick threaded with an olive. Repeat with the remaining ingredients to make 3 more sandwiches.

f) Wrap each sandwich halfway in wax paper (this will help catch all the juices) and serve.

24. Turkey Sliders with Sweet Potato

Makes 10 servings

INGREDIENTS
- 4 Applewood-smoked bacon strips, finely chopped
- 1-pound ground turkey
- 1/2 cup panko crumbs
- 2 large eggs
- 1/2 cup grated Parmesan cheese
- 4 tablespoons chopped fresh cilantro
- 1 teaspoon dried basil
- 1/2 teaspoon ground cumin
- 1 tablespoon soy sauce
- 2 large sweet potatoes
- Shredded Colby-Monterey Jack cheese

INSTRUCTIONS
a) In a large skillet, cook bacon over medium heat until crisp; drain on paper towels. Discard all but 2 tablespoons drippings. Set skillet aside. Combine bacon with next 8 ingredients until well mixed; cover and refrigerate at least 30 minutes.

b) Preheat oven to 425°. Cut sweet potatoes into 20 slices about 1/2 in. thick. Place slices on an ungreased baking sheet; bake until sweet potatoes are tender but not mushy, 30-35 minutes. Remove slices; cool on a wire rack.

c) Heat skillet with reserved drippings over medium-high heat. Shape turkey mixture into slider-sized patties. Cook sliders in batches, 3-4 minutes on each side, taking care not to crowd skillet. Add a pinch of shredded cheddar after flipping each slider the first time. Cook until a thermometer reads 165° and juices run clear.

d) To serve, place each slider on a sweet potato slice; dab with honey Dijon mustard. Cover with a second sweet potato slice. Pierce with toothpick.

25. White castle hamburger sliders

Yield: 10 servings

INGREDIENTS
- 2 pounds Lean Ground Beef
- ¼ cup Dry Minced Onion
- ¼ cup Hot Water
- 3 ounces Jar Strained Beef Baby Food
- ⅔ cup Clear Beef Broth
- 1 pack Hot Dog Buns

INSTRUCTIONS

a) Soak ¼ cup dry minced onions in ¼ cup hot water until soft while you mix 2 pounds ground beef with 3-ounce jar of strained beef baby food and ⅔ cup clear beef broth.

b) Keep patties uniform using ¼ cup meat mixture for each patty, flattened to ¼" and fried quickly in 1 T oil per patty on a hot griddle. Make 3 or 4 holes in patties while frying.

c) Cut hot dog buns in half. Cut off rounded ends. Fry 1 t onions under each patty as you turn to fry 2nd side. Slip each patty into bun with 2 dill pickle chips, mustard and catsup.

26. Cheeseburger Sliders

for 12 sliders

INGREDIENTS
- 2 lb. ground beef (910 g)
- 1 teaspoon salt
- 2 teaspoons pepper
- 2 teaspoons garlic powder
- ½ white onion, diced
- 6 slices cheddar cheese
- 12 dinner rolls, or Hawaiian sweet rolls
- 2 tablespoons butter, melted
- 1 tablespoon sesame seeds

INSTRUCTIONS

a) Preheat the oven to 350°F (175°C).
b) Combine the beef, salt, pepper, and garlic powder in a 9x13-inch (23x33-cm) rimmed baking dish, mixing thoroughly, then pressing into a flat, even layer. Bake for 20 minutes. Drain the liquid and set the cooked beef aside.
c) Slice the rolls in half lengthwise. Place the bottom half in the same baking dish. Place the cooked beef on the rolls, followed by the onions and cheese. Top with the remaining rolls.
d) Brush the tops of the rolls with melted butter and sprinkle the sesame seeds on top. Bake for 20 minutes, or until the bread is golden brown and the cheese is melted.
e) Slice into individual sliders, then serve.

27. Tempeh Reuben Sandwiches

Makes 2 sandwiches

INGREDIENTS
- 8 ounces tempeh
- 3 tablespoons vegan mayonnaise
- 1 tablespoon sweet pickle relish
- 1 green onion, minced
- 2 tablespoons olive oil
- Salt and freshly ground black pepper
- 4 slices rye or pumpernickel bread
- ¾ cup sauerkraut, well drained

INSTRUCTIONS
a) In a medium saucepan of simmering water, cook the tempeh for 30 minutes. Drain the tempeh and set aside to cool. Pat dry and cut into 1/4-inch slices.
b) In a small bowl, combine the mayonnaise, ketchup, relish, and green onion. Season with salt and pepper to taste, blend well, and set aside.
c) In a medium skillet, heat the oil over medium heat. Add the tempeh and cook until golden brown on both sides, about 10 minutes total. Season with salt and pepper to taste. Remove from the skillet and set aside.
d) Wipe out the skillet and set aside. Spread margarine on one side of each slice of bread. Place 2 slices of bread, margarine side down, in the skillet. Spread the dressing onto both slices of bread and layer with the fried tempeh and the sauerkraut.
e) Top each with the remaining 2 slices of bread, margarine side up. Transfer the sandwiches to the skillet and cook until lightly browned on both sides, turning once, about 2 minutes per side.
f) Remove the sandwiches from the skillet, cut in half, and serve immediately.

28. Tastes like Tuna Salad Sandwiches

Makes 4 sandwiches

INGREDIENTS:
- 1 1/2 cups cooked or 1 (15.5-ounce) can chickpeas, drained and rinsed
- 2 celery ribs, minced
- 1/4 cup minced onion
- 1 teaspoon capers, drained and chopped
- 1 cup vegan mayonnaise
- 2 teaspoons fresh lemon juice
- 1 teaspoon Dijon mustard
- 1 teaspoon kelp powder
- 4 lettuce leaves
- 4 slices ripe tomato
- Salt and pepper
- Bread

INSTRUCTIONS

a) In a medium bowl, coarsely mash the chickpeas. Add the celery, onion, capers, 1/2 cup of the mayonnaise, lemon juice, mustard, and kelp powder. Season with salt and pepper to taste. Mix until well combined. Cover and refrigerate at least 30 minutes to allow flavors to blend.

b) When ready to serve, spread the remaining 1/4 cup mayonnaise onto 1 side of each of the bread slices. Layer lettuce and tomato on 4 of the bread slices and evenly divide the chickpea mixture among them. Top each sandwich with the remaining slice of bread, mayonnaise side down, cut in half, and serve.

29. Sloppy Bulgur Sandwiches

Makes 4 sandwiches

INGREDIENTS:
- 1¾ cups water
- 1 cup medium-grind bulgur
- Salt
- 1 tablespoon olive oil
- 1 small red onion, minced
- 1/2 medium red bell pepper, minced
- 1 (14.5-ounce) can crushed tomatoes
- 1 tablespoon sugar
- 1 tablespoon yellow or spicy brown mustard
- 2 teaspoons soy sauce
- 1 teaspoon chili powder
- Freshly ground black pepper
- 4 sandwich rolls, halved horizontally

INSTRUCTIONS

a) In a large saucepan, bring the water to boil over high heat. Stir in the bulgur and lightly salt the water. Cover, remove from heat, and set aside until the bulgur softens and the water is absorbed, about 20 minutes.

b) Meanwhile, in a large skillet, heat the oil over medium heat. Add the onion and bell pepper, cover, and cook until soft, about 7 minutes. Stir in the tomatoes, sugar, mustard, soy sauce, chili powder, and salt and black pepper to taste. Simmer for 10 minutes, stirring frequently.

c) Spoon the bulgur mixture onto the bottom half of each of the rolls, top with the other half, and serve.

30. Garden Patch Sandwiches on Bread

Makes 4 sandwiches

INGREDIENTS:
- 1-pound extra-firm tofu, drained and patted dry
- 1 medium red bell pepper, finely chopped
- 1 celery rib, finely chopped
- 3 green onions, minced
- 1/4 cup shelled sunflower seeds
- 1/2 cup vegan mayonnaise
- 1/2 teaspoon salt
- 1/2 teaspoon celery salt
- 1/4 teaspoon freshly ground black pepper
- 8 slices whole grain bread
- 4 (1/4-inch) slices ripe tomato
- lettuce leaves

INSTRUCTIONS

a) Crumble the tofu and place it in a large bowl. Add the bell pepper, celery, green onions, and sunflower seeds. Stir in the mayonnaise, salt, celery salt, and pepper and mix until well combined.

b) Toast the bread, if desired. Spread the mixture evenly onto 4 slices of the bread. Top each with a tomato slice, lettuce leaf, and the remaining bread. Cut the sandwiches diagonally in half and serve.

31. Fruit-And-Nut Sandwiches

Makes 4 sandwiches

INGREDIENTS:
- 2/3 cup almond butter
- 1/4 cup agave nectar or pure maple syrup
- 1/4 cup chopped walnuts or other nuts of choice
- 1/4 cup sweetened dried cranberries
- 8 slices whole grain bread
- 2 ripe Bosc or Anjou pears, cored and thinly sliced

INSTRUCTIONS

a) In a small bowl, combine the almond butter, agave nectar, walnuts, and cranberries, stirring until well mixed.

b) Divide the mixture among the bread slices and spread evenly. Top 4 slices of the bread with the pear slices, spread side up. Place the remaining slices of bread on top of the pear slices, spread side down. Slice the sandwiches diagonally and serve at once.

32. Chicken and Waffles Grilled Cheese

INGREDIENTS:

- 16 oz. Mozzarella, sliced
- 12 slices pancetta, cut thin
- 1 Tablespoons maple syrup
- 1/2 cup mayonnaise
- 2 fresh peaches (or 1 small can of peaches, drained)
- 8 frozen waffles
- 2 Tablespoons softened butter
- 4 – 4 oz. boneless chicken breasts
- 1 cup flour
- 1 cup buttermilk ranch dressing
- 2 cups vegetable oil

INSTRUCTIONS

a) Cook pancetta in a nonstick pan until slightly crisp.
b) Mix syrup and mayonnaise together and set aside.
c) Slice peaches thin.
d) Lay out waffles and butter one side of each. Flip and spread mayonnaise mix on the non-buttered side of the waffles.
e) Flour chicken, then dip chicken in ranch dressing, then back into flour.
f) Bring vegetable oil to medium heat in a skillet and cook chicken until brown on both sides and internal temperature reaches 165 degrees.
g) On mayonnaise side of waffle, layer mozzarella, chicken, pancetta, peaches and finish with more mozzarella and another waffle.
h) In a nonstick pan on medium heat, cook for one minute, pressing down with a spatula. Flip and repeat until cheese is melted, and golden brown. Remove, cut and serve.

33. Grilled Ham and Cheese Waffle Sandwiches

Makes 4 servings

INGREDIENTS
- 8 frozen toaster waffles
- 1 tablespoon Dijon mustard (optional)
- ½ pound sliced deli ham
- ¼ pound Cheddar, thinly sliced
- 4 tablespoons unsalted butter

INSTRUCTIONS

a) Place 4 of the waffles on a work surface. Spread one side of each with the mustard (if using). Top with the ham, cheese, and the remaining waffles. Spread the top of each sandwich with 1/2 tablespoon of the butter. Melt the remaining butter in a large nonstick skillet over medium heat. Place the sandwiches in the skillet, buttered-side up.

b) Cook, pressing occasionally with the back of a spatula, until the cheese melts and the waffles are golden, 3 to 4 minutes on each side.

34. Pepperoni, Provolone and Pecorino Pita!

SERVES 4

INGREDIENTS:
- 4 pitas
- ½ cup roasted, peeled, and sliced red and/or yellow peppers
- 2 cloves garlic, chopped
- 4 ounces pepperoni, thinly sliced
- 4 ounces provolone cheese, diced
- 2 tablespoons freshly grated pecorino cheese
- 4 Italian or Greek pickled peppers such as pepperoncini, thinly sliced
- Olive oil for brushing pita

INSTRUCTIONS

a) Slit 1 side of each pita and open them to form pockets.
b) Layer the peppers, garlic, pepperoni, provolone, pecorino, and peppers into each pita and press to close. Brush the outsides lightly with olive oil.
c) Heat a heavy nonstick skillet over medium-high heat or use a sandwich maker or panini press. Place the sandwiches into the pan.
d) Reduce the heat to low and weight the sandwiches down, pressing as you brown them. Cook only until the cheese melts; you don't want the cheeses to brown and crisp, simply to hold all the fillings together.
e) Serve right away.

35. Grilled Cheddar, Chutney and Sausage

SERVES 4

INGREDIENTS:
- 1—2 savory spicy sausages, sliced diagonally
- 4 whole-wheat pitas, the pockets opened up
- 3—4 tablespoons sweet and spicy mango chutney
- 2 tablespoons chopped fresh cilantro
- 6—8 ounces mature Cheddar cheese, coarsely shredded
- 1 tablespoon olive oil for brushing bread
- 3 tablespoons shelled toasted sunflower seeds

INSTRUCTIONS

a) Brown the sliced sausages in a skillet over medium heat. Set them aside to drain on paper towels.

b) Arrange the pitas on a work surface. Spread 1 half of the inside with the chutney, then add the sausage, cilantro, and finally the cheese. Press lightly to close, and brush the outsides with olive oil.

c) Heat a heavy nonstick skillet over medium-high heat or use a panini press. Add the stuffed pitas and press lightly; reduce heat to medium or even medium-low. Cook on 1 side until lightly golden in spots and the cheese is melting; turn over and lightly brown on the second side. When cheese is melted, remove from the pan.

d) Serve right away, sprinkled with sunflower seeds, and offer additional chutney on the side for dabbing.

36. Curried Tofu "Egg Salad" Pitas

Makes 4 sandwiches

INGREDIENTS:
- 1-pound extra-firm tofu, drained and patted dry
- 1/2 cup vegan mayonnaise, homemade
- 1/4 cup chopped mango chutney, homemade
- 2 teaspoons Dijon mustard
- 1 tablespoon hot or mild curry powder
- 1 teaspoon salt
- 1/8 teaspoon ground cayenne
- 1 cup shredded carrot
- 2 celery ribs, minced
- 1/4 cup minced red onion
- 8 small Boston or other soft lettuce leaves
- 4 (7-inch) whole wheat pita breads, halved

INSTRUCTIONS

a) Crumble the tofu and place it in a large bowl. Add the mayonnaise, chutney, mustard, curry powder, salt, and cayenne, and stir well until thoroughly mixed.

b) Add the carrots, celery, and onion and stir to combine. Refrigerate for 30 minutes to allow the flavors to blend.

c) Tuck a lettuce leaf inside each pita pocket, spoon some tofu mixture on top of the lettuce, and serve.

37. Prosciutto and Taleggio with Figs on Mesclun

SERVES 4

INGREDIENTS:
- 8 very thin slices of sourdough bread or baguette
- 3 tablespoons extra-virgin olive oil, divided
- 3—4 ounces prosciutto, cut into 8 slices
- 8 ounces ripe Taleggio cheese, sliced into eight ¼-inch-thick pieces
- 4 big handfuls of salad spring mix (mesclun)
- 2 tablespoons chopped fresh chives
- 2 tablespoons chopped fresh chervil
- 1 tablespoon fresh lemon juice Salt
- Black pepper
- 6 ripe black figs, quartered
- 1—2 teaspoons balsamic vinegar

INSTRUCTIONS

a) Lightly brush the bread with a tiny amount of the olive oil and arrange on a baking sheet. 2 Preheat the oven to 400°F. Place the bread on the highest rack and bake about 5 minutes, or until they are just beginning to crisp. Remove and let cool, about 10 minutes.

b) When cool, wrap the prosciutto slices around the Taleggio slices and set each one atop a piece of bread. Set aside a moment while you prepare the salad.

c) Mix the greens with about 1 tablespoon of olive oil, the chives, and the chervil, then toss with the lemon juice, salt, and pepper to taste. Arrange on 4 plates and garnish with the fig quarters.

d) Brush the tops of the prosciutto-wrapped parcels with the remaining olive oil, then place in a large ovenproof skillet and bake for 5 to 7 minutes, or until the cheese begins to ooze and the prosciutto crisps around the edges.

e) Quickly remove the parcels and arrange on each salad, then shake the balsamic vinegar into the hot pan. Swirl so that it warms, then pour it over the salads and toasts. Serve right away.

38. <u>Fontina with Arugula, Mizuna and Pears</u>

SERVES 4

INGREDIENTS:
- 8 slices sourdough bread About 6 ounces bresaola, thinly sliced
- 6 —8 ounces nutty, flavorful, melting cheese such as fontina, Jarlsberg, or Emmentaler
- About 4 cups mixed baby arugula and mizuna, or other tender greens such as spring mix
- 2 ripe but firm pears, thinly sliced or julienned, tossed in a little lemon juice to keep them from browning
- 1 shallot, minced
- 1 tablespoon balsamic vinegar
- 2 tablespoons extra-virgin olive oil, plus more for brushing Salt
- Black pepper

INSTRUCTIONS

a) Arrange 4 pieces of the bread on a work surface and on 1 side lay the bresaola, then top with the cheese, and finish by topping with the other slices of sourdough. Press together lightly but firmly to seal.
b) Meanwhile, mix the greens in a bowl with the sliced pears. Set aside.
c) In a small bowl, mix the shallot with the balsamic vinegar and 2 tablespoons of olive oil, then season with salt and pepper to taste. Set aside.
d) Brush the sandwiches with a small amount of the olive oil. Heat a sandwich press or heavy nonstick skillet over medium-high heat, then place the sandwiches in the pan. You'll probably need to do this in 2 batches. Weight the sandwiches. Cook until the bread is crisp and golden, then turn over and repeat on the second side, until the cheese is melted.
e) Just before sandwiches are ready, toss the salad with the dressing. Distribute the salad among 4 plates. When the sandwiches are ready, remove from the pan, cut into quarters, and place 4 on each plate of salad.
f) Serve right away.

39. Chèvre Sandwiches in Salad

SERVES 4

INGREDIENTS:
- About ½ baguette, cut into 12 diagonal slices about ½-inch thick
- 2 tablespoons extra-virgin olive oil, or as needed
- 3 ounces goat cheese with a rind, such as Lezay, sliced ¼- to ½-inch thick
- Generous pinch of dried or fresh thyme leaves
- Black pepper
- 1 tablespoon red wine vinegar, divided
- About 6 cups mixed greens, such as spring mix, including a bit of young frisée and arugula
- 2 tablespoons chopped fresh parsley, chives, chervil, or a combination
- 1 tablespoon walnut oil
- ¼ cup walnut pieces

INSTRUCTIONS

a) Preheat the broiler.
b) Brush the baguette slices with a little of the olive oil, then set them on a baking sheet and broil for about 5 minutes, or until golden on 1 side only. Remove from the broiler.
c) Turn the toasted bread over and on the untoasted sides, place a slice or 2 of the goat cheese. The amount you use per sandwich will depend on how big your baguette slices are. Drizzle the tops with a tiny bit of olive oil, sprinkle on the thyme and black pepper, then shake a few drops of the vinegar over the cheeses.
d) Meanwhile, toss the salad with the chopped herbs and dress with the walnut oil and the remaining olive oil and vinegar, and sprinkle with the walnut pieces. Arrange on 4 big plates or in shallow soup bowls.
e) Place the goat cheese–topped toasts under the broiler and broil for about 5 minutes, or until the cheese is softened and the top just begins to bubble in places, the color of the cheese tinged golden brown.

f) Immediately place 3 hot goat cheese sandwiches on top of the dressed salad on each plate, and serve right away.

40. <u>**Sizzled Halloumi Sandwiches with Lime**</u>

SERVES 4

INGREDIENTS:
- 1 head butter or Boston Bibb lettuce, trimmed and separated into leaves
- 1 mild white onion, peeled and thinly sliced crosswise
- 4 tablespoons extra-virgin olive oil, divided
- 1 teaspoon white wine vinegar
- 3 large ripe tomatoes, cut into wedges
- Salt
- Black pepper
- ½ baguette, cut into 12 diagonal slices about ½-inch thick
- 12 ounces halloumi, sliced about ½ inch thick
- 2 limes, cut into wedges (or about 2 tablespoons fresh lime juice) A pinch dried oregano

INSTRUCTIONS

a) Preheat the broiler.
b) In a big bowl, toss together the lettuce and onion, then dress with about 2 tablespoons of the olive oil and the vinegar. Divide among 4 plates, then garnish each with tomato wedges; sprinkle salads with salt and pepper and set aside.
c) Brush the baguette slices with some of the olive oil, place on a baking sheet, and broil lightly on both sides. Set aside.
d) Arrange the halloumi on a baking sheet and brush with some olive oil. Broil on 1 side until browned in spots, then remove. Turn over each slice of cheese and place on top of a toast, then brush with olive oil again and return to the broiler. Broil until hot and lightly browned in spots.
e) Place 3 hot halloumi-topped toasts on each salad, squeeze lime juice over the halloumi, and let a little bit drizzle onto the salads. Sprinkle with oregano and serve.

41. **Truffled Toast and Arugula Salad**

SERVES 4

INGREDIENTS:
- 4 fairly thick slices pain au levain, each slice quartered
- About 2 teaspoons truffle oil, or to taste (the flavors of different truffle oils tend to vary widely)
- 2 ripe St. Marcellin cheeses (about 2 ½ ounces each)
- A pinch of salt
- About 8 ounces young arugula leaves (about 4 cups loosely packed)
- 2 tablespoons extra-virgin olive oil A few shakes of sherry vinegar

INSTRUCTIONS

a) Preheat the oven to 400°F.
b) Arrange the pieces of pain au levain on a baking sheet and lightly toast in the oven on both sides. Remove from the oven and sprinkle each with a bit of the truffle oil, then place about 1 tablespoon of the St. Marcellin cheese atop each toast.
c) Sprinkle the cheese lightly with a pinch of salt. Return to the oven for a few moments.
d) Meanwhile, arrange the arugula on 4 plates. Shake over each plate a bit of olive oil, a bit of truffle oil, and a few drops here and there of sherry vinegar. Don't toss, simply let the droplets lie on the plates.
e) Remove the cheese toasts from the oven after only 30 to 45 seconds. You do not want the cheese to melt completely or sizzle and go oily; you want it to simply become a bit warm and creamy.
f) Place 4 hot toasts onto each salad plate and serve immediately.

42. Ham, Cheese and Pineapple

SERVES 4

INGREDIENTS:
- 6—8 ounces turkey ham, coarsely chopped or cut into ribbons if already thinly sliced
- 3 tablespoons mayonnaise or as needed
- 4 thick slices fresh pineapple or 5 slices canned in its own juice
- 8 slices whole-wheat or wheat berry bread, thinly sliced
- About 12 to 15 slices of bread-and-butter pickles
- ½ onion, thinly sliced
- About 8 ounces Taleggio cheese (rind cut off), or sharp Cheddar cheese, sliced
- Extra-virgin olive oil for brushing bread

INSTRUCTIONS

a) In a small bowl, combine the turkey ham with the mayonnaise. Set it aside.

b) Dice or coarsely chop the pineapple and set it aside in a bowl. If using fresh, toss it with sugar to taste.

c) Lay out the bread slices. On 4 of them spread the pineapple. On the other 4, first place some of the pickles, then the turkey ham salad mixture, then some onion, and the Taleggio. Carefully top with the pineapple-topped bread slices to form sandwiches, and press together tightly. Brush each side lightly with the olive oil.

d) Heat a heavy nonstick skillet or panini press over medium-high heat. Place the sandwiches in the pan, browning and pressing, until the first side is crisp and golden and the cheese begins to melt; then using your spatula and possibly a little help from your hand, carefully turn the sandwiches over and cook on the second side, pressing as they brown.

e) When the sandwiches are crisp and lightly browned on both sides and the cheese is melted, remove from pan, cut into halves, and serve.

43. Ricotta Granola Crumble Grilled Cheese

INGREDIENTS:

- 15 oz. Ricotta
- 4 eggs
- 1/2 cup milk
- 8 slices pancetta
- 1 small red onion, sliced thin
- 5 Tablespoons softened butter, divided
- 1/2 cup of brown sugar
- 2 cups granola
- 8 slices cinnamon swirl bread

INSTRUCTIONS;

a) Whisk eggs with milk and set aside.
b) Add pancetta to preheated skillet and cook until crisp on medium high heat. Remove and set aside.
c) Put onions in the preheated skillet with 1 Tablespoons of butter. Once the onions start cooking, add brown sugar and cook until soft.
d) Add granola to a bowl and place next to the egg bowl.
e) Lay out slices of bread and spread butter on one side of each slice, using 2 Tablespoons butter total. On unbuttered side, spread a thick layer of ricotta.
f) Top ricotta with onions and pancetta and cover with remaining slice of bread. When closed, dip the entire sandwich in the egg mixture and transfer to the granola to completely coat all sides.
g) Preheat a nonstick pan and melt 2 Tablespoons butter using low to medium heat. Once butter is melted, add sandwich and cook for approximately 90 seconds, pressing down with a spatula. Flip and repeat until crisp. Remove, cut and serve.

44. Lasagna Grilled Cheese

INGREDIENTS:

- 16 oz. Mozzarella, sliced
- 15 oz. Ricotta
- 2 Tablespoons Grated Parmesan, divided 1/2 teaspoons black pepper
- 1 teaspoon fresh garlic, chopped
- 16 oz. ground beef
- 1 Tablespoons fresh basil, blended
- 8 slices Italian bread
- 2 Tablespoons softened butter
- 1 teaspoons garlic powder
- 16 oz. tomato sauce, divided

INSTRUCTIONS;

a) In a mixing bowl combine ricotta, 1 Tablespoons Parmesan, black pepper, garlic and basil. Set aside.
b) Heat a large skillet over medium-high heat. Cook and stir the ground beef until it is completely browned, approximately 7-10 minutes.
c) Lay out bread, butter one side and dust with garlic powder and remaining parmesan.
d) On the non-buttered side of 4 pieces, spread the ricotta mixture (about 1-2 Tablespoons on each piece). Layer the cooked ground beef on the ricotta, followed by the slices of mozzarella. On the remaining 4 pieces, spread 1-2 Tablespoons tomato sauce and place on the mozzarella to close sandwiches.
e) Move to a preheated pan on medium heat and cook for approximately 90 seconds, pressing down with a spatula. Flip and repeat until cheese is melted, and golden brown.
f) Remove, cut and serve with remaining tomato sauce to dip or cover sandwich.

45. Italian Classic Grilled Cheese

INGREDIENTS:

- 16 oz. Mozzarella, sliced
- 2 Tablespoons Grated Parmesan
- 4 sausage patties
- 1 green pepper, sliced thin
- 1 red pepper, sliced thin
- 1 small onion, sliced thin
- 1/4 cup olive oil
- 3/4 teaspoons garlic powder
- 8 slices Italian bread
- 2 Tablespoons softened butter

INSTRUCTIONS;

a) Cook the sausage patties to an internal temperature of 165 degrees F on the grill or in a grill pan.
b) Place sliced peppers and onions on a baking sheet. Lightly coat with oil and dust with garlic powder. Bake at 375 degrees F for 10 minutes until softened.
c) Lay out the slices of bread and spread butter on one side. Season buttered side with garlic powder and parmesan.
d) On the unbuttered side, layer a slice of mozzarella, sausage patty, peppers and onions and finish with more mozzarella.
e) Close sandwich and place in a nonstick pan on medium heat. Cook for approximately one minute, pressing down with a spatula.
f) Flip and repeat until cheese is melted, and golden brown. Remove, cut and serve.

46. Mediterranean Meatball Grilled Cheese

INGREDIENTS:

- 16 oz. Mozzarella, sliced
- 15 oz. Ricotta
- 2 Tablespoons Parmesan, divided
- 8 slices Italian bread, cut thick
- 2 Tablespoons softened butter
- 16 oz. tomato sauce
- 4 oz. pesto sauce or 12-16 fresh basil leaves, blended with 1/4 cup olive oil
- 2 sprigs fresh mint (approx. 12-16 leaves), chopped
- 8 – 2 oz. frozen meatballs (cooked), sliced

INSTRUCTIONS;

a) Lay out slices of bread. Spread butter on one side of each and dust 1 Tablespoons Parmesan onto butter sides.
b) Flip, and on non- buttered sides spread tomato sauce and a thick layer of ricotta cheese. Spread pesto onto cheese, followed by chopped mint and remaining Parmesan. Next, layer meatball slices and top with mozzarella.
c) Close sandwich and move to a medium pre-heated nonstick pan. Cook for approximately 90 seconds, pressing down with a spatula. Flip and repeat until cheese is melted, and golden brown. Remove, cut and serve.

47. Spinach Pesto and Avocado Grilled Cheese

INGREDIENTS:

- 16 oz. Mozzarella, sliced
- 15 oz. Ricotta
- 1 Tablespoons Parmesan, grated
- 2 Tablespoons fresh basil, finely chopped
- 8 slices marble rye bread
- 2 Tablespoons softened butter
- 1 - 8oz. package frozen spinach, thawed and drained
- 2 avocados (ripe), pitted and sliced

INSTRUCTIONS;

a) In small mixing bowl combine ricotta, pesto and Parmesan cheese and mix with fork until blended. Fold to make ricotta extra fluffy. Set aside.
b) Lay out the slices of bread and spread butter on one side of each piece.
c) Spread 1-2 Tablespoons of ricotta mixture on the unbuttered side of 4 slices.
d) Break up the spinach and lay out on the ricotta side, followed by the avocado and mozzarella.
e) Close sandwich and place in a medium preheated pan. Cook for approximately 90 seconds, pressing down with a spatula. Flip and repeat until cheese is melted, and golden brown. Remove, cut and serve.

48. Strawberry Basil Prosciutto Grilled Cheese

INGREDIENTS:

- 12 oz. Fresh Mozzarella, sliced
- 8 slices white bread, cut thick
- 2 Tablespoons softened butter
- 8 fresh strawberries (medium to large), sliced thin
- 12 fresh basil leaves, whole
- 8 slices prosciutto, cut thin
- 2 oz. balsamic glaze

INSTRUCTIONS;

a) Lay out slices of bread and butter one side of each.
b) On the unbuttered side, layer fresh mozzarella, strawberries, basil leaves and prosciutto. Drizzle with balsamic glaze; place remaining bread on top and transfer to a preheated nonstick pan. Cook for approximately one minute, pressing down with a spatula. Flip and repeat until golden brown.
c) Remove, drizzle with extra balsamic glaze over top if desired, cut and serve.

49. Ricotta Butter and Jam Grilled Cheese

INGREDIENTS:

- 15 oz. Ricotta
- 4 Tablespoons almond butter
- 2 teaspoons honey
- 12 slices pancetta (bacon can be substituted)
- 8 slices white bread, cut thick
- 2 Tablespoons softened butter
- 8 Tablespoons strawberry jam or jelly

INSTRUCTIONS

a) In a small mixing bowl, combine almond butter, honey and ricotta. Set aside.
b) Cook the pancetta until crisp.
c) Lay out the slices of bread and spread butter on one side of each piece. Flip the bread, and on the non-buttered side spread the ricotta/almond butter mixture, followed by jelly/ jam then pancetta.
d) Close the sandwich and move to a preheated pan on a low to medium heat.
e) Cook for approximately 90 seconds, pressing down with a spatula Flip and repeat until golden brown. Remove, cut and serve.

50. Buffalo Chicken Grilled Cheese

INGREDIENTS:

- 16 oz. Mozzarella, sliced
- 4 - 4 oz. boneless chicken breast, sliced 1/4 cup vegetable oil 1/2 cup hot sauce
- 1 celery stalk, small
- 1 carrot, small
- 8 slices white bread
- 2 Tablespoons softened butter
- 1 cup blue cheese dressing

INSTRUCTIONS

a) Lay out chicken on a plate. Coat both sides with the oil and place on a preheated grill or grill pan. Cook to an internal temperature of 165 degrees F, approx. 3 minutes on each side. Remove from grill and place in hot sauce. Set aside.
b) Cut celery into small pieces. Peel carrot and shave using a box grater.
c) Take 8 slices of bread, butter one side and spread blue cheese on the other side. On the blue cheese side, layer mozzarella, chicken, celery, carrots and finish with more mozzarella.
d) Top with the other piece of bread and place in a nonstick pan on medium heat. Cook for approximately one minute, pressing down with a spatula.
e) Flip and repeat until cheese is melted, and golden brown. Remove, cut and serve.

51. Veggie Pizza Grilled Cheese

INGREDIENTS:

- 16 oz. Mozzarella, sliced
- 15 oz. Ricotta
- 4 Tablespoons Parmesan, divided
- 1 eggplant, small
- 2 red peppers
- 1 zucchini, large
- 3/4 cup olive oil, divided
- 1 teaspoon fresh garlic, chopped
- 4 - 8 in. pizza crusts, precooked
- 1 sprig fresh rosemary, stemmed and finely chopped

INSTRUCTIONS

a) Pre-heat oven to 375 degrees F.
b) Peel the eggplant and cut into 1/4 inch slices. Cut peppers and zucchini into 1/4 inch slices. Lay vegetables out on a baking sheet and lightly coat with olive oil. Bake in oven at 375 degrees for 15-20 minutes until softened.
c) In a mixing bowl, add ricotta, garlic and half of the Parmesan and mix with fork until blended. Fold to make ricotta extra fluffy. Set aside.
d) Lay out the pre-baked pizza crust and lightly coat with remaining olive oil. Sprinkle one side with the chopped rosemary and remaining Parmesan. Flip, and on the unseasoned side spread the ricotta mixture. Set aside.
e) Once vegetables are done, assemble sandwich by placing eggplant, zucchini and peppers on the ricotta half of the crust followed by the mozzarella. Close and place in a preheated skillet or nonstick pan at low to medium heat. Make sure the pan is larger than the crust.
f) Cook for approximately 90 seconds, pressing down with a spatula. Flip and repeat until golden brown and cheese is fully melted. Remove, cut and serve.

52. Cheddar and Sourdough Grilled cheese

Yield 1 serving

INGREDIENTS:

- 2 pieces sourdough bread
- 1 ½ tablespoons unsalted butter
- 1 ½ tablespoons mayonnaise
- 3 slices cheddar cheese

INSTRUCTIONS

a) On a cutting board, butter each piece of bread with butter on one side.
b) Flip the bread over and spread each piece of bread with mayonnaise.
c) Place the cheese on the buttered side of one piece of bread. Top it with the second piece of bread, mayonnaise side out.
d) Heat a nonstick pan over medium low heat.
e) Place the sandwich on the pan, mayonnaise side down.
f) Cook for 3-4 minutes, until golden brown.
g) Using a spatula, flip the sandwich over and continue cooking until golden brown, about 2-3 minutes.

53. Grilled cheese sandwich

Yield 2

INGREDIENTS:

- 4 slices white bread
- 3 tablespoons butter, divided
- 2 slices Cheddar cheese

INSTRUCTIONS

a) Preheat skillet over medium heat.
b) Generously butter one side of a slice of bread. Place bread butter-side-down onto skillet bottom and add 1 slice of cheese.
c) Butter a second slice of bread on one side and place butter-side-up on top of sandwich.
d) Grill until lightly browned and flip over; continue grilling until cheese is melted.
e) Repeat with remaining 2 slices of bread, butter and slice of cheese.

54. **Spinach and Dill Havarti Sandwich**

SERVES 4

INGREDIENTS:
- 8 thin slices of Italian country-style white bread
- 3-4 tablespoons white truffle paste or other truffle or truffle porcini
- 4 ounces Taleggio cheese, sliced
- 4 ounces fontina cheese, sliced Soft butter for spreading on bread

INSTRUCTIONS

a) Lightly spread 1 side of each slice of bread with truffle paste. Top 4 of the slices with the Taleggio and fontina, then top each with another truffle paste–spread bread.
b) Lightly spread butter on the outside of each sandwich, then heat a panini press or a heavy nonstick skillet over medium-high heat.
c) Brown the sandwiches, turning once or twice, until the bread is crisp and golden and the cheese has melted.
d) Serve immediately, fragrant with truffle and oozing melted cheese, cut into quarters or dainty bars.

55. Grilled Jack on Rye with Mustard

SERVES 4

INGREDIENTS:
- 2 tablespoons green olive tapenade
- 3 tablespoon mild Dijon mustard
- 8 slices seeded rye bread
- 8-10 ounces Jack cheese, or other mild white cheese (such as Havarti or Edam), sliced
- Olive oil for brushing bread

INSTRUCTIONS

a) Mix the tapenade with the mustard in a small bowl.
b) Lay out the bread and spread 4 of the slices on one side only with the tapenade mustard to taste. Top with the cheese and the second piece of bread, then press together well.
c) Lightly brush the outside of each sandwich with the olive oil, then brown in a sandwich maker, panini press, or heavy nonstick skillet, weighted down to press the sandwiches as they brown.
d) Cook over medium-high heat until lightly crisped on the outside and the cheese is melting within.
e) Serve hot and sizzling, golden brown.

56. Radicchio and Roquefort on Pain au Levain

SERVES 4

INGREDIENTS:
- 6-8 ounces Roquefort cheese
- 8 thin slices pain au levain or sourdough bread
- 3 tablespoons toasted coarsely chopped pecans
- 4-8 large leaves radicchio
- Olive oil for brushing, or soft butter for spreading on bread

INSTRUCTIONS

a) Spread the Roquefort cheese evenly on all 8 slices of bread.
b) Sprinkle 4 of the cheese-spread slices with pecans, then top each with a piece or 2 of the radicchio; use enough of the leaves to peek over the edges. Top each with a second piece of cheese-spread bread and press together to seal. Brush the outsides with the oil or butter.
c) Heat a heavy nonstick skillet or panini press over medium-high heat. Place the sandwiches in the pan, working in 2 batches, depending on size of the pan. Weight down according to the Tip on, and cook, turning once or twice until the bread is crisp and the cheese has melted.
d) Serve immediately, cut into halves or quarters.

57. Garlic Grilled Cheese on Rye

SERVES 4

INGREDIENTS:
- 4 large, thick slices of sourdough rye bread
- 4 cloves garlic, halved
- 4-6 ounces feta cheese, thinly sliced or crumbled
- 2 tablespoons chopped fresh chives or green onion
- About 6 ounces thinly sliced or shredded mild white melting cheese such as Jack, medium Asiago, or Chaume

INSTRUCTIONS

a) Preheat the broiler.
b) Lightly toast the bread on a baking sheet under the broiler. Rub both sides with garlic. Chop any leftover garlic and set it aside for a moment.
c) Lay the feta over the top of the garlic-rubbed toasts, sprinkle with leftover chopped garlic, then with chives, and top with the second cheese.
d) Broil until the cheese melts and sizzles, lightly browning in spots, and the edges of the toast are crisp and brown.
e) Serve right away, hot and oozing.

58. British Melted Cheese and Pickle

SERVES 4

INGREDIENTS:
- 4 slices hearty flavorful white or whole-wheat bread
- About 3 tablespoons Pickle, coarsely chopped
- 6-8 ounces strong mature Cheddar cheese or English Cheshire, sliced

INSTRUCTIONS

a) Preheat the broiler.
b) Arrange the bread on a baking sheet. Lightly toast under the broiler, then remove and spread the pickle generously on the lightly toasted bread; top with the cheese and pop under the broiler until the cheese melts.

59. Fresh Mozzarella, Prosciutto and Fig Jam

SERVES 4

INGREDIENTS:
- 4 soft French or Italian rolls (or half-baked if available)
- 10—12 ounces fresh mozzarella, thickly sliced
- 8 ounces prosciutto, thinly sliced
- ¼-½ cup fig jam or fig preserves, to taste
- Soft butter for spreading on bread

INSTRUCTIONS

a) Split each roll, and layer with the mozzarella and prosciutto. Spread the top slices with the fig jam, then close up.
b) Lightly butter the outside of each sandwich.
c) Heat a heavy nonstick skillet or panini press over medium-high heat. Place the sandwiches in the pan, working in two batches depending on the size of the pan. Press or close the grill and brown, turning once or twice, until the bread is crisp and the cheese has melted. Though the rolls start off as round, once pressed they are considerably flatter and can be easily turned, albeit carefully.

60. Rare Roast Beef with Blue Cheese

SERVES 4

INGREDIENTS:
- 4 soft sourdough or sweet rolls
- 10-12 ounces blue cheese, at room temperature for easier spreading
- 8-10 ounces rare roast beef, thinly sliced
- Handful watercress leaves
- Soft butter for spreading on bread

INSTRUCTIONS

a) Split each roll, then spread generously with blue cheese on each side. Into each roll, layer the roast beef, then the watercress leaves, and close up again, pressing well to seal.
b) Lightly butter the outside of each sandwich.
c) Heat a heavy nonstick skillet, or panini press, over medium-high heat.
d) Place the sandwiches in the pan, working in 2 batches, depending on the size of the pan.
e) Weight down and cook, turning once or twice until the bread is crisp and the cheese has melted.

61. Red Leicester with Onion

SERVES 4

INGREDIENTS:
- 8 thin slices of soft whole wheat, sprouted wheat berry, dill, or hearty white such as potato bread
- ½ medium onion, peeled and very thinly sliced crosswise
- 10-12 ounces mild Cheddar-type cheese
- Olive oil for brushing or soft butter for spreading on bread
- A mild, spunky, very interesting mustard of choice

INSTRUCTIONS

a) Lay the slices of bread out. Top 4 pieces of bread with a single layer of onion, then enough cheese to cover the bread and onion completely. Top each with the remaining slices of bread to form sandwiches, and press together well.
b) Brush the outside of the sandwiches with olive oil or spread with soft butter.
c) Heat a heavy nonstick skillet or sandwich press over medium-high, then add the sandwiches and reduce the heat to medium. Place a weight on top if using a skillet, lowering the heat if it threatens to burn. Check every so often; when golden and flaked brown on one side, turn them over, weight down, and brown the second side.
d) Serve immediately, cut into wedges or triangles, accompanied by mustard for dabbing.

62. Spinach and Dill Havarti on Bread

SERVES 4

INGREDIENTS:
- 2 cloves garlic, chopped
- 2 tablespoons extra-virgin olive oil, divided
- 1 cup cooked, chopped spinach, drained and squeezed dry
- 8 slices multigrain bread or 1 piece of focaccia, about 12 × 15 inches, cut horizontally
- 8 ounces dill Havarti, sliced

INSTRUCTIONS

a) In a heavy nonstick skillet over medium-low heat, warm the garlic in 1 tablespoon of the olive oil, then add the spinach and cook together a moment or two to warm through.
b) On 4 slices of the bread (or the bottom layer of the focaccia), arrange the cheese, then top with the spinach and a second piece of bread (or the top of the focaccia).
c) Press together to seal well, then lightly brush the outside of the sandwiches with the remaining olive oil.
d) Brown the sandwiches in the skillet, weighting them, or in a panini press over medium-high heat. Cook until lightly crisped and golden on one side, then turn and brown the second side. When cheese is melted the sandwich is ready.
e) Serve immediately, cut on the diagonal.

63. Open-Faced Grilled Cheddar and Dill Pickle

SERVES 4

INGREDIENTS:
- 4 slices good-quality white bread
- 6-8 ounces mature Cheddar cheese, thinly sliced
- 1-2 sweet gherkin or kosher dill pickles, thinly sliced

INSTRUCTIONS

a) Preheat the broiler.
b) Lightly toast the bread under the broiler, then top each slice with a little cheese, the pickle, and more cheese. Broil until the cheese melts and the edges of the bread get crisp and browned.
c) Serve right away, cut into quarters.

64. Harry's Bar Special

MAKES 12; SERVES 4

INGREDIENTS:
- 6 ounces Gruyère, Emmentaler, or other Swiss cheese, shredded coarsely
- 2-3 ounces diced smoked ham
- A generous pinch of dry mustard
- A few shakes of Worcestershire sauce
- 1 tablespoon whipping cream or sour cream, or enough to hold it all together
- 8 very thin slices of dense white bread, crusts cut off
- Olive oil for brushing or soft butter for spreading on bread

INSTRUCTIONS

a) In a medium bowl, combine the cheese with the smoked ham, mustard, and Worcestershire sauce. Mix well, then mix in the cream, adding just enough for it to form a firm mixture and hold together.
b) Spread the cheese-and-ham mixture very thickly onto 4 pieces of the bread and top with the other 4. Press together well and cut sandwiches into 3 fingers each.
c) Brush the outside of the sandwiches with olive oil, then brown over medium-high heat in a heavy nonstick skillet, pressing them down using your spatula as they cook. When lightly crisped on the first side, turn them over and brown the second side.
d) Serve hot, right away.

65. Casse Croûte of Blue Cheese and Gruyère

SERVES 4

INGREDIENTS:
- 1 baguette, split lengthwise and slightly hollowed out
- 2-3 tablespoons soft butter for spreading on bread
- 1-2 tablespoons dry white wine
- 3-4 cloves garlic, chopped
- 8-10 ounces flavorful blue cheese
- 8-10 ounces Gruyère
- Grating of nutmeg

INSTRUCTIONS

a) Preheat the broiler.
b) Spread the baguette halves lightly on the inside with the butter, then sprinkle with some of the white wine and some of the garlic. Layer on the cheeses, ending with a layer of the Gruyère, and finishing with a grating of nutmeg, the remaining garlic, and a few drops more of the wine.
c) Broil the sandwiches until the cheese melts and sizzles and the edges of the bread crisp and brown.
d) Cut into pieces a few inches long, and serve right away.

66. Crisp Truffled Comté with Black Chanterelles

SERVES 4

INGREDIENTS:
- 1 ounce fresh or ½ ounce dried black chanterelle mushrooms
- 6 tablespoons unsalted butter
- ¼ cup mushroom or vegetable broth
- 2 tablespoons black truffle oil, or to taste

Sandwiches
- 1 baguette, thinly sliced on a slight diagonal
- 8 ounces Comté cheese, sliced about $1/8$-inch thick and cut to fit the small slices of baguette
- 1—2 tablespoons extra-virgin olive oil for brushing bread
- 1—2 cloves garlic, minced
- 1—2 tablespoons chopped fresh chives or flat-leaf parsley

INSTRUCTIONS

a) To make the sautéed chanterelles: If using fresh mushrooms, wash and dry them, then chop finely. If using dried mushrooms, pour the mushroom broth, heated to just boiling, over the mushrooms to rehydrate. Leave to sit, covered, for about 30 minutes or until soft and pliable. Remove from the liquid and squeeze dry, reserving the liquid for the cooking below. Chop the rehydrated mushrooms and proceed as with fresh.

b) Heat the butter over medium heat in a heavy nonstick skillet; when melted and nutty brown, add the mushrooms and sizzle a few moments in the hot butter. Pour in the broth and cook over medium-high heat until the liquid is almost completely evaporated, 5 to 7 minutes. Remove from the heat and spoon into a bowl. Leave to cool a few minutes, then add the truffle oil, and stir well, mixing it in vigorously.

c) Lay out the baguette slices; smear half of them with the truffled mushroom mixture, then top with slices of the cheese and finally the remaining pieces of baguette. Press together well; the sandwiches, being small with a relatively dry filling, tend to fall

apart. Once the sandwiches brown, however, the cheese melts and holds them together.
d) Brush the outside of each sandwich lightly with the olive oil. Heat a heavy nonstick skillet over medium-high heat and then add the sandwiches, working in batches as necessary. Top with a <u>weight</u> and reduce the heat to medium or medium-low. Brown the sandwiches, turning once or twice, until the bread is crisp and golden and the cheese has melted. Sprinkle with some of the garlic and chives, and serve.
e) Sprinkling on the garlic just before you remove it from the pan keeps the pungent and strong flavor of the raw garlic, so that each little sandwich tastes like a cheese-and-truffle-filled garlic crouton. Repeat with remaining sandwiches, removing any leftover garlic from the pan so it doesn't burn on the next round of sandwich browning.

67. Goat Cheese Toasts with Spices

MAKES 12; SERVES 4

INGREDIENTS:
- 12 thin baguette slices
- Extra-virgin olive oil
- 3—4 ounces slightly aged goat cheese
- About ¼ teaspoon ground cumin
- ½ teaspoon thyme
- ¼-½ teaspoon paprika
- About 1/8 teaspoon ground coriander
- 2 cloves garlic, chopped
- 1—2 tablespoons chopped fresh cilantro

INSTRUCTIONS

a) Preheat broiler.
b) Brush the baguette slices with olive oil, arrange in a single layer on a baking sheet, and lightly toast under the broiler on each side.
c) Top the toasted baguette slices with the cheese, then sprinkle with the cumin, thyme, paprika, coriander, and chopped garlic. Drizzle with olive oil and broil until the cheese melts slightly, and browns in spots.
d) Sprinkle with the cilantro and serve right away.

68. Roquefort Sandwiches and Beet Marmalade

MAKES 8; SERVES 4
GINGERED BEET MARMALADE

INGREDIENTS:
- 3 medium-large red beets (16 to 18 ounces total), whole and unpeeled
- 1 onion, quartered, plus ½ onion, chopped
- ½ cup red wine
- About ¼ cup red wine vinegar
- About 2 tablespoons sugar
- 2 tablespoons raisins or diced dried figs
- About ½-teaspoon chopped peeled fresh ginger
- Pinch of five-spice powder, cloves, or allspice

Sandwiches
- 16 very thinly sliced diagonal pieces of stale baguette, or thinly sliced stale ciabatta
- 6 ounces Roquefort cheese
- About 1 tablespoon olive oil for brushing bread
- About 2 cups (3 ounces) watercress

INSTRUCTIONS

a) Preheat the oven to 375°F.
b) **To make the beet marmalade:** Place the beets, quartered onion, and red wine in a baking pan just large enough to fit them with a few inches of space in-between. Cover the pan with aluminum foil, then bake for an hour, or until the beets are tender. Remove, uncover, and leave to cool.
c) When cool, slip the skin from the beets, then dice in ¼ to $1/8$-inch pieces. Coarsely chop the cooked onion and combine it with the diced roasted beets and the cooking juices from the pan in a saucepan along with the chopped raw onion, vinegar, sugar, raisins, ginger, and several tablespoons of water.
d) Bring to a boil and cook over medium-high heat until the onion is softened, and most of the liquid has evaporated. Do not let it burn. Remove from heat and adjust flavorings with more sugar

and vinegar. Season very subtly—a pinch only—with five-spice powder. Set aside. Makes about 2 cups.

e) **To make the sandwiches:** Lay out 8 of the baguette slices and spread each thickly with Roquefort cheese. Top each with the remaining slices of baguette and press together well to hold. Brush each side of the little sandwiches with a small amount of olive oil.

f) Heat a heavy nonstick skillet over medium-high heat and place the sandwiches in it. Reduce heat to medium-low or medium. Cook the sandwiches until they turn a crisp golden on the first side, press together lightly with the spatula, then turn and lightly brown the other side.

g) Serve the crisp hot little sandwiches on a plate, garnished with a tuft or two of watercress and a generous spoonful of the beet marmalade.

69. Bocadillo from the Island of Ibiza

SERVES 4
TUNA AND RED PEPPER SPREAD

INGREDIENTS:
- 6 ounces chunk white-meat tuna, packed in olive oil, drained
- 1 red pepper, roasted, peeled, and chopped (from a jar is fine)
- ½ onion, finely chopped
- 4—6 tablespoons mayonnaise
- 1 tablespoon extra-virgin olive oil
- 1—2 teaspoons paprika
- A few drops of fresh lemon
- juice
- Salt
- Black pepper

Sandwiches
- 8 slices sun-dried tomato bread
- 8 ounces aged Gouda cheese, Jack, or white Cheddar
- Olive oil for brushing bread

INSTRUCTIONS

a) To make the tuna mixture: Break up the tuna with a fork in a medium bowl, then mix with the red pepper, onion, mayonnaise, extra-virgin olive oil, paprika, lemon juice, salt, and pepper. Adjust amounts of mayonnaise to reach a nice thick consistency.

b) To make the sandwiches: Arrange 4 slices of the bread and top each with a quarter of the cheese. Top with the tuna mixture, then with the remaining bread.

c) Brush the outside of the sandwiches lightly with the olive oil. Heat a heavy nonstick skillet over medium-high heat and add the sandwiches.

d) Weight them down with the bottom of a heavy <u>frying pan</u>, not to press them but to hold the tops on and keep them flat while the cheese melts. Lower the heat to medium, and cook on the first side until the bread is crisp and golden, then turn over and repeat.

e) Lift the weighting pan every so often to check on the situation with the cheese.
f) When it melts—and you can tell this because a little bit will ooze out—and the bread is gold and crisp, remove from the pan. If the bread is getting too dark before the cheese melts, reduce the heat.
g) Serve right away, hot and sizzling-crisp.

70. Club Grilled Sandwich

SERVES 4

INGREDIENTS:
- 3 tablespoons mayonnaise
- 1 tablespoon capers, drained
- 8 thick slices bacon
- 8 thin slices pain au levain, cut from half a large loaf (about 10 inches long, 5 inches wide)
- 8 ounces Beaufort, Comté, or Emmentaler cheese, sliced
- 2 ripe tomatoes, sliced
- 2 poached, roasted, or grilled boneless chicken breasts, sliced
- Olive oil for brushing bread
- About 2 cups arugula leaves
- About 12 leaves fresh basil

INSTRUCTIONS

a) In a small bowl, combine the mayonnaise with the capers. Set aside.
b) Cook the bacon in a heavy nonstick skillet until it is crisp and brown on both sides. Remove from the pan and drain on absorbent paper towels.
c) Arrange 4 pieces of the bread on a work surface and top each with a layer of cheese, then a layer of tomatoes, bacon, and finally the chicken.
d) Generously spread the caper mayonnaise on the 4 remaining slices of bread and top each sandwich. Press to close tightly.
e) Brush the outsides lightly with olive oil.
f) Heat a heavy nonstick skillet or panini press over medium-high heat. Add the sandwiches, working in two batches if you need to. Weight down the sandwiches lightly, reduce heat to medium, and cook until the bottom of the bread is browned in spots and the cheese has melted somewhat.
g) Turn over carefully, using your hands to help stabilize the sandwiches on the spatula if they are threatening to fall apart. Brown on the second side, without a weight, but pressing on the sandwiches a bit to consolidate them and hold them together.

h) Remove from the pan, open the tops of all 4 sandwiches, and stuff in a handful of arugula and a few basil leaves, then close them all up.
i) Cut in halves and serve right away.

71. Welsh Rarebit with Poached Egg

SERVES 4

INGREDIENTS:
- 4 large eggs
- A few drops of white wine vinegar
- 4 slices whole-wheat or sourdough bread, or 2 halved English muffins
- About 2 tablespoons soft butter
- 12 ounces sharp Cheddar or Cheshire cheese, coarsely shredded
- 1—2 green onions, thinly sliced
- 1—2 teaspoons ale or lager (optional)
- ½ teaspoon whole-grain mustard and/or several pinches powdered dry mustard
- Several generous shakes of Worcestershire sauce
- Several shakes of cayenne pepper

INSTRUCTIONS

a) Poach the eggs: Crack each egg and place in a cup or ramekin. Bring a deep skillet filled with water to a boil; lower the heat and keep it at a bubbling simmer. Do not salt the water, but rather, add a few shakes of vinegar. Slip each egg into the lightly simmering water.

b) Cook the eggs until the whites are firm and the yolks still runny, 2 to 3 minutes. Remove with a slotted spoon and place on a plate to drain excess water.

c) Preheat the broiler.

d) Lightly toast the bread under the broiler and lightly butter it.

e) Arrange the bread on a baking sheet. Top each piece with 1 of the poached eggs.

f) In a medium bowl, mix together the Cheddar, green onions, ale, mustard, Worcestershire sauce, and cayenne pepper. Gently spoon the cheese mixture evenly over the poached eggs, taking care not to break the yolks.

g) Broil the cheese-and-egg-topped toasts until the cheese melts into a gooey sauce-like mixture, and the edges of cheese and toast alike crisp and brown. Serve right away.

72. A Hot Muffaletta

SERVES 4

INGREDIENTS:
- 4 soft French rolls
- Extra-virgin olive oil
- A few shakes here and there of red wine vinegar
- 4—6 cloves garlic, chopped
- 3—4 teaspoons capers, drained
- 2—3 large pinches of dried oregano, crumbled
- ½ cup chopped or diced roasted red pepper
- 4 mild pickled peppers, such as Greek or Italian, sliced
- ½ red or other mild onion, very thinly sliced
- ½ cup pimiento-stuffed green olives, sliced
- 1 large tomato, thinly sliced
- 4 ounces dried salami, thinly sliced
- 4 ounces ham, smoked turkey
- 8 ounces thinly sliced provolone cheese

INSTRUCTIONS

a) Open the rolls and pull out a bit of their fluffy insides. Sprinkle each cut side with olive oil and vinegar, then with the garlic, capers, and oregano. On 1 side of each roll, layer the red pepper, pickled peppers, onion, olives, tomato, salami, ham, and finally the cheese. Close up tightly and press together well to help seal.

b) Heat a heavy nonstick skillet over medium-high heat and lightly brush the outside of each roll with olive oil. Place the sandwiches in the pan and <u>weight down</u>, or place them in a panini press.

c) Cook until golden brown on one side, then turn and brown the second side. Sandwiches are ready when they are crisply golden and the cheese has oozed a bit and crisped in places. Cut into halves, and eat right away.

73. Cuban Sandwich

SERVES 4

INGREDIENTS:

Mojo sauce
- 2 tablespoons extra-virgin olive oil
- 8 cloves garlic, thinly sliced
- 1 cup fresh orange juice and/or grapefruit juice
- ½ cup fresh lime juice and/or lemon juice
- ½ teaspoon ground cumin Salt
- Black pepper

Sandwiches
- 1 soft baguette or 4 soft long French rolls, split
- Soft butter or olive oil for brushing bread
- 6 ounces thinly sliced boiled or honey-roast ham
- 1 cooked chicken breast, about 6 ounces, thinly sliced
- 8 ounces flavorful cheese such as Gouda, manchego, or Edam, sliced
- 1 dill, kosher dill, or sweet pickle, thinly sliced
- About 4 leaves butter or Boston Bibb lettuce
- 2—3 medium, ripe tomatoes, sliced

INSTRUCTIONS

a) To make the Mojo Sauce: Gently heat the olive oil and garlic in a small heavy skillet until the garlic is lightly golden but not browned, about 30 seconds. Add the citrus juices, cumin, salt, and pepper to taste, and remove from the heat. Let cool, taste, and adjust for seasoning. Lasts up to 3 days in the refrigerator. Makes 1 ½ cups.

b) Preheat the broiler.

c) To make the sandwiches: Pull out a little of the fluffy insides of each roll. Discard the pulled-out bread or reserve it for another use. Brush both sides of the rolls with a small amount of soft butter or olive oil. Lightly toast under the broiler on each side, then remove from the heat.

d) Splash a little of the mojo sauce onto the cut sides of the bread, then layer with the ham, chicken, cheese, and pickle. Close up well and press together to help seal and lightly brush outsides of the sandwiches with olive oil.

e) Heat a heavy nonstick skillet or panini press over medium-high heat, and brown the sandwiches, <u>weighting them down</u>. You want to press the sandwiches as flat as possible. Cook until lightly crisped on the outside and the cheese begins to melt. Squish the sandwiches with the spatula when you turn them to help press them flat, too.

f) When sandwiches are crisp and browned, remove from the pan. Open up, add the lettuce and tomato, and serve right away, with extra mojo on the side.

74. Parisian Grilled Cheese

SERVES 4

INGREDIENTS:
- 8 slices firm, flavorful good-quality white or French bread
- 4 thin slices boiled or baked ham or turkey ham
- 2 tablespoons unsalted soft butter
- 4 ounces Gruyère-type cheese

INSTRUCTIONS

a) Preheat the broiler.
b) Arrange 4 slices of the bread on a baking sheet, then top with the ham and the remaining slices of bread to make sandwiches. Butter each sandwich on the outside, then place under the broiler until lightly golden, turn, and brown on the second side.
c) Sprinkle cheese all over the top of one side of the sandwiches, then return to the broiler for a few moments or until the cheese melts and bubbles a bit here and there. Eat right away with green salad nestled next to it.

75. Bocadillo from the Island of Ibiza

SERVES 4

INGREDIENTS:
- 4 large soft flattish French or Italian-style rolls
- 6—8 cloves garlic, halved
- 4—6 tablespoons extra-virgin olive oil
- 1 tablespoon tomato paste
- 2—3 large ripe tomatoes, thinly sliced
- Generous sprinkling of dried oregano
- 8 thin slices Spanish jamon or similar ham such as prosciutto
- About 10 ounces mild and melting, yet flavorful cheese, such as manchego, Idiazábal, Mahon, or a California cheese such as Ig Vella's semi secco or Jack
- Mixed Mediterranean olives

INSTRUCTIONS

a) Preheat the broiler.
b) Cut open the rolls and lightly toast on each side under the broiler.
c) Rub the garlic on the cut side of each piece of bread.
d) Drizzle the garlic-rubbed bread with the olive oil and brush the outsides with a bit more of the oil. Spread lightly with the tomato paste, then layer the sliced tomatoes and their juices onto the rolls, pressing in the tomato paste and tomatoes so that the juices are absorbed into the bread.
e) Sprinkle with crumbled oregano, then layer with the ham and cheese. Close up and press together well, then brush lightly with olive oil.
f) Heat a heavy nonstick skillet pan or panini press over medium-high heat, then add the sandwiches. If using a pan, weight the sandwiches down.
g) Lower the heat to medium-low and cook until lightly crisped on the outside and the cheese begins to melt. Turn over and brown on the second side.
h) Cut in halves, and serve immediately, with a handful of mixed olives alongside.

76. Tomato and Mahon Cheese on Olive Bread

MAKES 4

INGREDIENTS:
- 10—12 fresh, small sage leaves
- 3 tablespoons unsalted butter
- 1 tablespoon extra-virgin olive oil
- 8 slices country bread
- 4 ounces prosciutto, thinly sliced
- 10—12 ounces full-flavored mountain cheese such as fontina, aged Beaufort, or Emmentaler
- 2 cloves garlic, chopped

INSTRUCTIONS

a) In a heavy nonstick skillet, stir the sage leaves, butter, and olive oil together over medium-low heat until the butter melts and foams.

b) Meanwhile, lay out 4 slices of bread, top with the prosciutto, then the fontina, then a sprinkle of garlic. Place the remaining bread on top and press together firmly.

c) Gently place the sandwiches in the hot sage butter mixture; you may need to do them in several batches or use 2 pans. Weight with a heavy frying pan on top to press the sandwiches down. Cook until lightly crisped on the outside and the cheese begins to melt. Turn over and brown on the second side.

d) Serve sandwiches hot and crisp, cut into diagonal halves. Either discard the sage leaves or nibble them up, crisp and browned.

77. Emmentaler and Pear Sandwich

SERVES 4

INGREDIENTS:
- 8 thin slices pain au levain, sourdough, or sour pumpernickel
- 4 ounces Emmentaler cheese, thinly sliced
- 1 ripe but firm pear, unpeeled and very thinly sliced
- 4 ounces Appenzell cheese, thinly sliced
- Several pinches of cumin seeds Soft butter or olive oil for brushing bread

INSTRUCTIONS

a) Arrange 4 slices of the bread on a work surface, then top with a layer of the Emmentaler cheese, then the pear, then some Appenzell cheese, and a sprinkling of cumin seeds. Top each sandwich with a second slice of bread and press together firmly to seal.

b) Spread the outside of each sandwich lightly with butter. Heat a heavy nonstick skillet or sandwich press over medium-high heat. Put a weight on the sandwiches. Brown, turning once or twice, until the bread is crisp and golden and the cheese has melted.

c) Serve right away.

78. Grilled Pumpernickel and Gouda

SERVES 4

INGREDIENTS:

Parsley-tarragon mustard
- 3 tablespoons whole-grain mustard
- 3 tablespoons mild Dijon mustard
- 2 tablespoons chopped fresh flat-leaf parsley
- 1 tablespoon chopped fresh tarragon
- 1 small clove garlic, minced
- A few drops of red or white wine vinegar, to taste

Sandwiches
- 8 slices soft dark pumpernickel bread
- 8 ounces aged Gouda, manchego, or similar nutty aged cheese
- Soft butter or olive oil for brushing bread

INSTRUCTIONS

a) To make the Parsley-Tarragon Mustard: Combine the whole-grain and Dijon mustards in a small bowl and stir in the parsley, tarragon, and garlic. Add a few drops of vinegar to taste and set aside. Makes about $1/3$ cup.

b) To make the sandwiches: Arrange 4 slices of the bread on a work surface. Add a layer of the cheese, then top with the second piece of bread. Press together and lightly spread or brush the outsides with the butter.

c) Heat a heavy nonstick skillet or panini press over medium-high heat and add the sandwiches. Weight with a second frying pan and reduce the heat to medium-low. Cook until the first side is crisp and golden, then turn and cook the second side until the cheese is melted.

d) Serve immediately, with the Parsley-Tarragon Mustard on the side, to dab on as desired.

79. Smoked Turkey, Taleggio and Gorgonzola

SERVES 4

INGREDIENTS:
- 1 soft, flat, airy Italian bread, such as ciabatta, or 4 soft Italian/French rolls; if half-baked are available, choose these
- 6 ounces Gorgonzola cheese, thinly sliced or crumbled coarsely
- 8 ounces smoked turkey, thinly sliced
- 1 medium or 2 small crisp but flavorful apples, cored, unpeeled, and very thinly sliced
- 6 ounces Taleggio, Teleme, Jack, or a tomme de montagne cheese, cut into 4 slices (Whether to leave the Taleggio rind or cut it off is up to you; the rind has a slightly strong flavor which some love, some emphatically do not.)
- Olive oil for brushing bread

INSTRUCTIONS

a) Cut the bread into 4 equal-sized pieces. Slice each piece of bread horizontally, leaving 1 side connected if possible.
b) Open up the 4 pieces of bread. On 1 side layer the Gorgonzola, smoked turkey, and sliced apple in equal amounts. Top with the Taleggio and close the sandwiches up tightly, pressing firmly to close.
c) Brush the sandwiches, top and bottom, with olive oil, then heat a heavy nonstick skillet over medium-high heat. Place the sandwiches in the hot pan and reduce the heat at once to very low. Weight on top, or use a sandwich press or panini press.
d) Cook until they are golden brown and toasted, then turn over and lightly brown the second sides. Check every so often to be sure that the bread is not burning.
e) Serve as soon as both sides are crisp and the cheese is melted.

80. Melted Jarlsberg on Sourdough

SERVES 4

INGREDIENTS:
- 8 medium-thick slices sourdough bread
- 8 ounces Jarlsberg or a mild melting cheese such as Jack
- 2 roasted red peppers, sliced, or 3 to 4 tablespoons chopped roasted red peppers
- 2 cloves garlic, thinly sliced
- 2 teaspoons chopped fresh rosemary leaves, or to taste
- Olive oil for brushing bread

INSTRUCTIONS

a) Arrange 4 slices of bread on a work surface and top with the cheese, then add the red peppers, garlic, and rosemary. Top with the remaining slices of bread and press together gently. Brush the outside of each sandwich lightly with the oil.

b) Heat a heavy nonstick skillet or sandwich press over medium-high heat and add the sandwiches, working in several batches if need be. Lower the heat to medium-low, browning the sandwiches slowly (press with the spatula to help crisp), until lightly crisped on the outside and the cheese begins to melt. Turn over and repeat on second side.

c) Serve each sandwich cut into halves or quarters.

81. Torta of Chicken, Queso Fresco, and Gouda

SERVES 4

INGREDIENTS:
- 2 sage/herbed sausages (about 14 ounces), either pork, turkey, or vegetarian
- 6 ounces shredded Jack or medium Asiago cheese
- 1—2 tablespoons (about 2 ounces) freshly grated aged cheese such as Parmesan, locatelli Romano, or dry Jack
- 2 green onions, thinly sliced
- 2—3 teaspoons sour cream Pinch of cumin seeds Tiny pinch of turmeric Dab of brown mustard
- Pinch of cayenne pepper or a few drops hot pepper sauce
- 8 thin slices whole-grain (such as wheat berry, sunflower seed, or sprouted wheat) bread
- 2—3 tablespoons extra-virgin olive oil
- 3 cloves garlic, thinly sliced
- 1—2 Moroccan-style preserved lemons, rinsed well and sliced into slivers or chopped
- 1—2 teaspoons finely chopped fresh flat-leaf parsley

INSTRUCTIONS

a) Roughly dice the sausages, then brown them quickly over medium heat in a small nonstick skillet. Remove from the pan, place on paper towels, and leave to cool. Leave the pan on the stove and turn off the heat.

b) In a medium bowl, mix together the 2 cheeses with the green onions, sour cream, cumin seeds, turmeric, mustard, and cayenne pepper. When the sausage is cool, mix it into the cheese.

c) Pile 4 slices of the bread with the cheese-and sausage mixture, then top with a second piece of bread. Pat down well and press lightly but firmly so that the sandwich will hold together.

d) Reheat the pan over medium-high heat and add about half the olive oil and garlic, then push the garlic to one side and add 1 or 2 sandwiches, however many the pan will hold. Cook until lightly crisped on one side and the cheese begins to melt.

e) Turn over and cook the second side until it is golden brown. Remove to a plate and repeat with the other sandwiches, garlic, and oil. You may either discard the lightly browned garlic or nibble on it; whichever you do, remove it from the pan before it blackens as it will give a bitter flavor to the oil if it burns.
f) Serve the sandwiches right away, piping hot, cut into triangles, and sprinkled with the preserved lemon and chopped parsley.

82. Panini of Eggplant Parmigiana

SERVES 4

INGREDIENTS:
- ¼ cup extra-virgin olive oil, or as desired, divided
- 1 medium eggplant, sliced ½ to ¾ inch thick
- Salt
- 4 large softish rolls, sourdough or sweet
- 3 cloves garlic, chopped
- 8 big fresh basil leaves
- About ½ cup ricotta cheese
- 3 tablespoons freshly grated Parmesan, pecorino, or locatelli Romano cheese
- 6—8 ounces fresh mozzarella cheese
- 4 ripe juicy tomatoes, thinly sliced (including their juices)

INSTRUCTIONS

a) Arrange the eggplant slices on a cutting board and sprinkle generously with salt. Let sit for about 20 minutes or until droplets of moisture appear on the surface of the eggplant. Rinse it off well, then pat dry the eggplant.

b) Heat 1 tablespoon of the oil in a heavy nonstick skillet over medium heat. Add as much of the eggplant that will fit in a single layer and not crowd each other. Brown the eggplant slices, moving them around so that they brown and cook through but do not burn.

c) Turn and cook on the second side until that side too is lightly browned and the eggplant is tender when pierced with a fork. When eggplant is cooked, remove to a plate or pan, and continue adding eggplant until they are all cooked. Set aside for a few minutes.

d) Open up the rolls and pull a little of the fluffy insides out, then sprinkle each cut side with chopped garlic. On 1 side of each roll, place a slice or 2 of eggplant, then top with a leaf or 2 of basil, some ricotta cheese, a sprinkle of Parmesan, and a layer of mozzarella. Finish with sliced tomatoes; close up and press gently to seal together.

e) Heat the same skillet over medium-high heat or use a panini press, and lightly brush the sandwiches with a bit of olive oil on the outsides. Brown or grill the sandwiches, pressing as they brown and crisp.
f) When the first side is browned through, turn over and brown the second side until the cheese is melted. Serve right away.

83. Grilled Eggplant and Chaumes

SERVES 4

INGREDIENTS:

RED CHILI AIOLI
- 2—3 cloves garlic, minced
- 4—6 tablespoons mayonnaise Juice of ½ lemon or lime (about 1 tablespoon or to taste)
- 2—3 teaspoons chili powder 1 teaspoon paprika
- ½ teaspoon ground cumin Large pinch dried oregano leaves, crushed
- 2 tablespoons extra-virgin olive oil
- Several shakes smoky chile sauce such as Chipotle Tabasco, or Buffalo
- 2 tablespoons coarsely chopped fresh cilantro
- 1 eggplant, cut crosswise into ¼- to ½-inch-thick slices Olive oil
- 4 soft white or sourdough rolls, or 8 slices of country-style white or sourdough bread
- ¾ cup marinated roasted red and/or yellow peppers
- About 12 ounces semi-soft but flavorful cheese

INSTRUCTIONS

a) To make the Red Chili Aioli: In a small bowl, combine the garlic with the mayonnaise, lemon juice, chili powder, paprika, cumin, and oregano; stir well to combine. With your spoon or a whisk, beat in the olive oil, adding the oil a few teaspoons at a time and beating it until incorporated into the mixture before adding the rest.

b) When smooth, shake in smoked chile sauce to taste, and finally stir in the cilantro. Cover and chill until ready to use. Makes about 1/3 cup.

c) To prepare the eggplant, lightly brush the eggplant slices with olive oil and heat a heavy nonstick skillet over medium-high heat. Pan brown the eggplant slices on each side until they are lightly browned and tender when pierced with a fork. Set aside.

d) To make the sandwiches: Lay out the open soft rolls and layer the red chili aioli generously on the insides. Layer eggplant slices on one side of the rolls, then the peppers, then a layer of the cheese. Close up and press together well. Lightly brush the outside of each sandwich with olive oil.

e) Heat the skillet again over medium-high heat, then add the sandwiches and reduce the heat to medium-low. Weight down the sandwiches, and cook for a few minutes. When the bottom bread is golden and slightly browned in places, turn over and cook the other side, similarly weighted.

f) **5** When that side too is golden and crisp, the cheese should be melted and gooey; it may be oozing out a bit and crisping as it does. (Don't discard these delicious crispy bits, just plop them onto each plate along with the sandwich.)

g) Remove the sandwiches to plates; cut into halves and serve.

h) Smoky Bacon and Cheddar with Chipotle Relish

i) Smoky chipotle relish, a smear of tangy mustard, meaty smoky bacon, and strong pungent Cheddar—there's nothing subtle about this big-flavored sandwich. Try the chipotle relish on a hamburger, too! A glass of cerveza with a wedge of lime on the side comes close to perfection.

84. Mushrooms and Melted Cheese on Pain au Levain

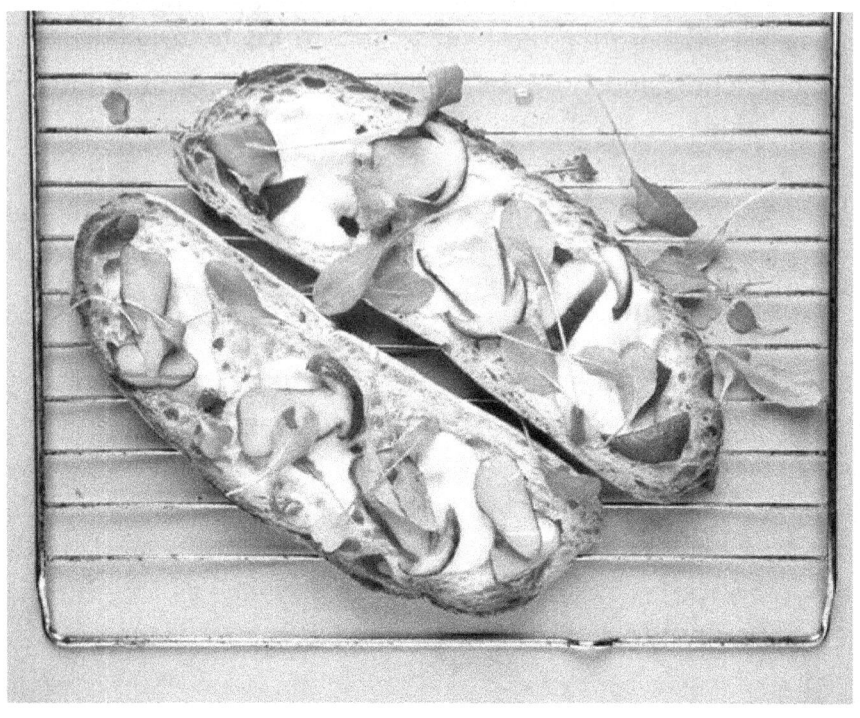

SERVES 4

INGREDIENTS:
- 1—1½ ounces dry porcini or cèpes,
- About ½ cup heavy cream
- Salt
- A few grains of cayenne pepper
- A few drops of fresh lemon juice
- ½ teaspoon cornstarch, mixed with 1 teaspoon water
- 8 slices pain au levain or other French bread
- About 1 tablespoon soft butter for spreading on bread
- 2 cloves garlic, finely chopped
- 8—10 ounces sliced pecorino, fontina, or Mezzo Secco cheese
- 4 tablespoons freshly grated Parmesan cheese
- About ¼ cup finely chopped fresh chives

INSTRUCTIONS

a) In a heavy saucepan, combine the mushrooms and 2 cups of water. Bring to a boil, then reduce the heat and simmer until the liquid is nearly evaporated and the mushrooms are softened, 10 to 15 minutes.

b) Stir in the cream and return to the heat for a few minutes, then season with salt, just a grain or two of cayenne, and just a drop or two of lemon juice.

c) Stir in the cornstarch mixture and warm over medium-low heat until it thickens. It should thicken as soon as the edges begin to bubble. Because cream can vary in thickness, there is no way of knowing exactly how much cornstarch you will need.

d) Once thick enough, leave mixture at room temperature to cool. It will thicken further as it cools. You want a thick spreadable consistency.

e) Lay out all of the bread and brush 1 side of each slice very lightly with the butter. Turn them all over, then on 4 of them, sprinkle the garlic. Top with the slices of pecorino, some of the chunks of mushrooms from the sauce, and a sprinkling of Parmesan.

f) On the other 4 pieces of bread (unbuttered side), spread the mushroom sauce thickly. Close the sandwiches up tightly. The buttered sides will be on the outside.
g) Heat a heavy nonstick skillet over medium-low heat. Add the sandwiches, 1 or 2 at a time, depending on the size of the pan, and weight them with a heavy frying pan).
h) Cook until the bread is golden and lightly browned in places, delightfully crisp, and the cheese is starting to ooze. Turn over and repeat until the second side is as golden and crisp as the first, adding the chopped garlic to the pan for the final minute or so of cooking. The cheese should be runny by now, with a few bits oozing out and lightly crisping at the edge of the crust.
i) Place on a plate, cut into halves or quarters, and sprinkle the plate with chives. Eat right away. There is nothing as sodden as a cold grilled cheese sandwich.

85. Sicilian Sizzled Cheese with Capers and Artichokes

SERVES 4

INGREDIENTS:
- 4—6 marinated artichoke hearts, sliced
- 4 thick slices country bread, either sweet or sourdough
- 12 ounces provolone, mozzarella, manouri, or other mild and meltable cheese, shredded
- 2 tablespoons extra-virgin olive oil
- 4 cloves garlic, very thinly sliced or minced
- About 2 tablespoons red wine vinegar
- 1 tablespoon capers in brine, drained
- 1 teaspoon crumbled dried oregano
- Several grindings black pepper
- 1—2 teaspoons chopped fresh flat-leaf parsley

INSTRUCTIONS

a) Preheat the broiler.
b) Arrange the artichokes on the bread and place on a baking sheet, then top with the cheese.
c) In a heavy nonstick skillet, heat the olive oil over medium-high heat, then add the garlic and lightly brown. Add the red wine vinegar, capers, oregano, and black pepper, and cook a minute or two, or until the liquid reduces to about 2 teaspoons. Stir in the parsley. Spoon over the cheese-topped bread.
d) Broil until the cheese melts, bubbles, and turns golden in spots. Eat right away.

86. Scaloppine and Pesto sandwich

SERVES 4

INGREDIENTS:
- Two 4- to 5-ounce boneless skinless chicken breasts or cutlets of pork, turkey, or veal
- Salt
- Black pepper
- 2 tablespoons extra-virgin olive oil, divided
- 3 cloves garlic, chopped, divided
- 2 zucchinis, very thinly sliced and patted dry
- 2 tablespoons basil pesto, or to taste
- 2 tablespoons grated Parmesan, grana, or locatelli Romano cheese
- 4 soft sourdough rolls, or four 6-inch pieces of focaccia, halved
- 8–10 ounces mozzarella, domestic or Danish fontina, or Jack cheese, sliced

INSTRUCTIONS

a) Pound the meat with a meat mallet; if it is thick, slice the chicken into very thin pieces. Sprinkle with salt and pepper.

b) Heat a heavy nonstick skillet over medium-high heat, then add 1 tablespoon of the oil, the meat, and finally about half of the garlic. Brown the meat quickly on 1 side, then the other, then remove from the pan, and pour any bits of juice and garlic over the meat.

c) Return the pan to medium-high heat, and add another teaspoon or so of the oil. Sauté the zucchini until it is just tender. Remove to a bowl; season with salt and pepper. When it is cool, stir in the remaining garlic, the pesto, and the Parmesan cheese. Leave mixture to cool in a bowl; rinse and dry the pan.

d) With your fingers, tear out a little bit of the fluffy insides of each roll to make way for the filling. Heat the pan again over medium-high and lightly toast the cut sides of each roll. You will have to press them a bit; they may tear a little, but that is okay. They'll go back together again as they are browned and pressed with their filling in place.

e) Into half of each roll, stuff several tablespoons of the zucchini-pesto mixture, then top with a layer of the meat and the mozzarella. Close up and press together tightly to seal well.
f) Brush the remaining oil on the outsides of the sandwiches. Heat the pan again over medium-high heat. Weight sandwiches to help press them down and keep them together. Reduce the heat to medium-low and cook until the first side is crisp and golden and the cheese begins to melt. Turn over and repeat.
g) Serve when the sandwiches are crisply golden and the cheese is melting seductively.

87. Mozzarella, Basil Piadine

SERVES 4

INGREDIENTS:
- 4 piadine or medium (12-inch) flour tortillas
- 3—4 tablespoons tomato paste
- 1 large ripe tomato, thinly sliced
- 1—2 cloves garlic, chopped
- 4—6 ounces fresh mozzarella cheese, sliced
- About 12 leaves Thai or Vietnamese basil (or ordinary basil)
- About 3 ounces Gorgonzola cheese, sliced or crumbled
- 2—3 tablespoons freshly grated Parmesan or other grating cheese such as Asiago or grana
- Extra-virgin olive oil for drizzling

INSTRUCTIONS

a) Preheat the broiler.
b) Lay the piadine out on 1 or 2 baking sheets and spread them with a bit of the tomato paste, then layer with a small amount of the tomato, and sprinkle with the garlic. Top with the mozzarella, basil, and Gorgonzola, sprinkle with the Parmesan, then drizzle with olive oil.
c) Broil, working in batches if necessary, until the cheese melts and the sandwiches are sizzling hot. Serve right away.

88. Quesadillas on Pumpkin Tortillas

SERVES 4

INGREDIENTS:
- 2 large mild green chiles such as Anaheim or poblano, or 2 green bell peppers
- 1 onion, chopped
- 2 cloves garlic, chopped
- 1 tablespoon extra-virgin olive oil
- 1-pound lean ground beef
- $1/8$–$1/4$ teaspoon ground cinnamon, or to taste
- ¼ teaspoon ground cumin Pinch of ground cloves or allspice
- $1/3$ cup dry sherry, or dry red wine
- ¼ cup raisins
- 2 tablespoons tomato paste
- 2 tablespoons sugar
- A few shakes of red wine or sherry vinegar
- Salt
- Black pepper
- A few shakes of cayenne, or Tabasco if using bell peppers instead of chiles
- ¼ cup coarsely chopped almonds
- 2–3 tablespoons coarsely chopped fresh cilantro, plus extra for garnishing
- 8 pumpkin tortillas
- 6–8 ounces mild cheese such as Jack, manchego, or Mezzo Secco
- Olive oil for brushing tortillas
- About 2 tablespoons sour cream for garnishing

INSTRUCTIONS

a) Roast the chiles or peppers over an open flame until they are charred lightly and evenly all over. Place in a plastic bag or bowl, and cover. Set aside for at least 30 minutes, as the steam helps separate the skins from the flesh.

b) Prepare the picadillo: Sauté the onion and garlic in the olive oil over medium heat until softened, then add the beef and cook together, stirring and breaking up the meat as you cook. When the meat is browned in spots, sprinkle with the cinnamon, cumin, and cloves and continue cooking and stirring.

c) Add the sherry, raisins, tomato paste, sugar, and vinegar. Cook together for about 15 minutes, stirring every so often; if it seems dry, add a little water or more sherry. Season with salt, pepper, and cayenne, and adjust the sugar and vinegar to taste. Add the almonds and cilantro and set aside.

d) Remove the skin, stems, and seeds from the peppers, then cut the peppers into strips.

e) Lay out 4 of the tortillas and spread with the picadillo. Add the roasted pepper strips, then a layer of the cheese, and top each with a second tortilla. Press down firmly to hold them together.

f) Heat a heavy nonstick skillet over medium-high heat. Brush the outsides of the quesadillas lightly with olive oil and add them to the pan, working in batches.

g) Lower the heat to medium-low, brown on one side, then carefully turn over using the spatula with guidance from your hand if needed. Cook on the second side until golden in spots and the cheese is melted.

h) Serve immediately, cut into wedges, garnished with a dollop of sour cream and cilantro.

89. Grilled Sheep Cheese Quesadillas

SERVES 4

INGREDIENTS:
- 8 big flour tortillas
- 1 tablespoon chopped fresh tarragon
- 2 large ripe tomatoes, thinly sliced
- 8–10 ounces slightly dry sheep cheese
- Olive oil, for brushing tortillas

INSTRUCTIONS

a) Lay the tortillas out on a work surface, sprinkle with the tarragon, and layer with the tomatoes. Top with the cheese and cover each with a second tortilla.

b) Brush each sandwich with olive oil, and heat a heavy nonstick skillet or flat grill over medium heat. Working 1 at a time, cook the quesadilla on 1 side; when it is flecked lightly with golden brown and the cheese is melting, turn it over and cook the second side, pressing as it cooks to flatten it.

c) Serve immediately, cut into wedges.

90. Toast with Strawberries and Cream Cheese

SERVES 4

INGREDIENTS:
- 8 medium-thick slices soft, sweet white bread, such as challah or brioche
- 8—12 tablespoons (about 8 ounces) cream cheese (low fat is fine)
- About ½ cup strawberry preserves
- 1 cup (about 10 ounces) sliced strawberries
- 2 large eggs, lightly beaten
- 1 egg yolk
- About ½ cup milk (low fat is fine)
- A dash vanilla extract
- Sugar
- 2—4 tablespoons unsalted butter
- ½ teaspoon fresh lemon juice
- ½ cup sour cream
- Several sprigs fresh mint, thinly sliced

INSTRUCTIONS

a) Spread 4 slices of the bread thickly with the cream cheese, tapering a bit towards the sides so that the cream cheese doesn't seep out in the cooking, then spread the other 4 slices of bread with the preserves.
b) Scatter a light layer of strawberries over the top of the cream cheese.
c) Top each piece of cheese-spread bread with a preserve-spread piece of bread. Press gently but firmly to seal.
d) In a shallow bowl, combine the eggs, egg yolk, milk, vanilla extract, and about 1 tablespoon of sugar.
e) Heat a heavy nonstick skillet over medium-high heat. Add the butter. Dip each sandwich, 1 at a time, into the bowl with the milk and egg. Let it soak in a moment or 2, then turn over and repeat.
f) Place the sandwiches into the hot pan with the melted butter and let them cook to a golden brown. Turn over and lightly brown the second sides.

g) Meanwhile, combine the remaining strawberries with sugar to taste and the lemon juice.
h) Serve each sandwich as soon as it's done, garnished with a spoonful or 2 of the strawberries and a dollop of the sour cream.
i) Sprinkle them with some of the mint as well.

91. <u>Bread Pudding Sandwiches</u>

SERVES 4

INGREDIENTS:
- ¾ cup packed light brown sugar
- ¼ cup sugar, divided
- 5—6 cloves
- $1/_8$ teaspoon ground cinnamon, plus extra for shaking on top
- 1 large tangy apple such as Granny Smith, unpeeled and thinly sliced
- ¼ cup raisins
- ½ teaspoon vanilla extract
- 8 thick (¾- to 1-inch) slices French bread
- 6—8 ounces mild meltable cheese such as Jack, or a very mild white Cheddar, sliced
- ½ cup slivered blanched almonds or pine nuts
- About 3 tablespoons butter
- 1 tablespoon olive oil

INSTRUCTIONS

a) In a heavy-bottomed saucepan, combine the brown sugar with 2 tablespoons of the sugar, the cloves, and the cinnamon. Add 2 cups of water and stir to mix well.

b) Place over a medium-high heat and bring to a boil, then reduce the heat to medium-low, until the liquid forms a light bubbling simmer. Cook for 15 minutes, or until it forms a syrup. Add the apple slices and raisins, then cook a further 5 minutes. Remove from the heat and add the vanilla.

c) Arrange the slices of bread on a work surface. Spoon hot syrup over each piece of bread, several tablespoons per piece. Carefully turn each piece over and spoon hot syrup over the second sides. Leave for about 30 minutes.

d) Spoon a bit more syrup onto the bread, again about one tablespoon or so per slice of bread. The bread will become quite soft and risk falling apart as it absorbs the sweet syrup, so take care when handling it. Leave a further 15 minutes or so.

e) Place one slice of cheese on top of 4 slices of the soaked bread. Top each with about ¼ of the apples, raisins, and a sprinkling of almonds (reserve some for the end). Top with the remaining slices of bread to form 4 sandwiches. Press together.

f) Heat a heavy nonstick skillet over medium-high heat, then add about 1 tablespoon each of butter and olive oil. When butter foams and browns, add the sandwiches. Reduce the heat to medium and cook, pressing gently with the spatula. Adjust the heat as the sandwiches brown, lowering it as needed to keep the sugar in the syrup browning but not burning.

g) Turn the sandwiches several times, adding more butter to the pan, taking care that the sandwiches do not fall apart as you turn them. Press every so often, until the outsides of the sandwiches are browned and crisp and the cheese has melted.

h) A minute or 2 before they reach this state, toss the remaining almonds into the pan and let them lightly toast and brown. Sprinkle the sandwiches and the almonds with the remaining 2 tablespoons sugar.

i) Serve immediately, each sandwich sprinkled with the toasted almonds.

92. Grain and cheese burger

Yield: 4 Servings

INGREDIENTS:
- 1½ cup Mushrooms, chopped
- ½ cup Green onions, chopped
- 1 tablespoon Margarine
- ½ cup Rolled oats, regular
- ½ cup Brown rice, cooked
- ⅔ cup Shredded cheese, mozzarella
- Or cheddar
- 3 tablespoons Walnuts, chopped
- 3 tablespoons Cottage or ricotta cheese
- Low fat
- 2 large Eggs
- 2 tablespoons Parsley, chopped
- Salt, pepper

INSTRUCTIONS

a) In a 10 to 12-inch nonstick frying pan over medium heat, cook mushrooms and green onions in margarine until vegetables are limp, about 6 minutes. Add oats and stir for 2 minutes.

b) Remove from heat, let cool slightly, then stir in cooked rice, cheese, walnuts, cottage cheese, eggs, and parsley. Add salt and pepper to taste. On an oiled 12X15 inch baking sheet shape into 4 patties, each ½ inch thick.

c) Broil 3 inches from heat, turning once, 6 to 7 minutes total. Serve on bread with mayo, onion rings, and lettuce.

93. Black angus burger with cheddar cheese

Yield: 1 Servings

INGREDIENTS:
- 2 pounds Ground Angus beef
- 3 Grilled poblano peppers, seeded and; slice in thirds
- 6 slices Yellow cheddar cheese
- 6 Hamburger rolls
- Baby red oak lettuce
- Pickled red onions
- Poblano Pepper Vinaigrette
- Salt and freshly ground black pepper

INSTRUCTIONS

a) Prepare a wood or charcoal fire and let it burn down to embers.

b) In a large mixing bowl season angus beef with salt and pepper. Refrigerate until ready to use. When ready to use, form into 1-inch thick disks.

c) Grill for five minutes on each side for medium rare. During the last five minutes top with cheddar cheese. When finished grilling, on one half of the roll place the burger and top with baby red oak, poblano peppers, vinaigrette and pickled red onions. Serve immediately.

94. Grilled American cheese and tomato sandwich

Yield: 4 servings

INGREDIENTS:
- 8 slices White bread
- Butter
- Prepared mustard
- 8 slices American cheese
- 8 slices Tomato

INSTRUCTIONS

a) For each sandwich, butter 2 slices of white bread. Spread the unbuttered sides with prepared mustard and place 2 slices of American cheese and two slices of tomato between the bread, buttered sides out.
b) Brown in a skillet on both sides or grill until cheese melts.

95. Grilled apple and cheese

Yield: 2 Servings

INGREDIENTS:
- 1 small Red Delicious apple
- ½ cup 1% low-fat cottage cheese
- 3 tablespoons Finely chopped purple onion
- 2 Sourdough English muffins, split and toasted
- ¼ cup Crumbled blue cheese

INSTRUCTIONS

a) Core apple, and slice crosswise into 4 (¼-inch) rings; set aside.
b) Combine cottage cheese and onion in a small bowl, and stir well. Spread about 2-½ tablespoons cottage cheese mixture on each muffin half.
c) Top each muffin half with 1 apple ring; sprinkle crumbled blue cheese evenly over apple rings. Place on a baking sheet.
d) Broil 3 inches from heat for 1-½ minutes or until blue cheese melts.

96. Grilled blue cheese sandwiches with walnuts

Yield: 1 servings

INGREDIENTS:
- 1 cup Crumbled blue cheese; (about 8 ounces)
- ½ cup Finely chopped toasted walnuts
- 16 slices Whole wheat bread; trimmed
- 16 smalls Watercress sprigs
- 6 tablespoons Butter; (3/4 stick)

INSTRUCTIONS
a) Divide cheese and walnuts equally among 8 bread squares. Top each with 2 watercress sprigs.
b) Sprinkle with pepper and top with remaining bread squares, making 8 sandwiches total. Press together gently to adhere.
c) Melt 3 tablespoons butter in large nonstick griddle or skillet over medium heat. Cook 4 sandwiches on griddle until golden brown and cheese melts, about 3 minutes per side.
d) Transfer to cutting board. Repeat with remaining 3 tablespoons butter and 4 sandwiches.
e) Cut sandwiches diagonally in half. Transfer to plates and serve.

97. Grilled cheddar cheese and ham sandwiches

Yield: 1 Servings

INGREDIENTS:
- ¼ cup (1/2 stick) butter; room temperature
- 1 tablespoon Dijon mustard
- 2 teaspoons Minced fresh thyme
- 2 teaspoons Minced fresh parsley
- 8 6x4-inch slices country-style bread; (about 1/2-inch thick)
- ½ pounds Cheddar cheese; thinly sliced
- ¼ pounds Thinly sliced smoked ham
- ½ small Red onion; thinly sliced
- 1 large Tomato; thinly sliced

INSTRUCTIONS

a) Mix first 4 **INGREDIENTS** in bowl. Season with salt and pepper. Arrange 4 bread slices on work surface.
b) Divide half of cheese equally among bread slices. Top with ham, then onion, tomato and remaining cheese. Top sandwiches with remaining bread. Spread herb butter on outside of sandwich tops and bottoms.
c) Heat large nonstick skillet over medium heat. Add sandwiches and cook until bottoms are golden, about 3 minutes. Turn sandwiches over, cover skillet and cook until cheese melts and bread is golden, about 3 minutes.

98. Party Grilled cheese and bacon

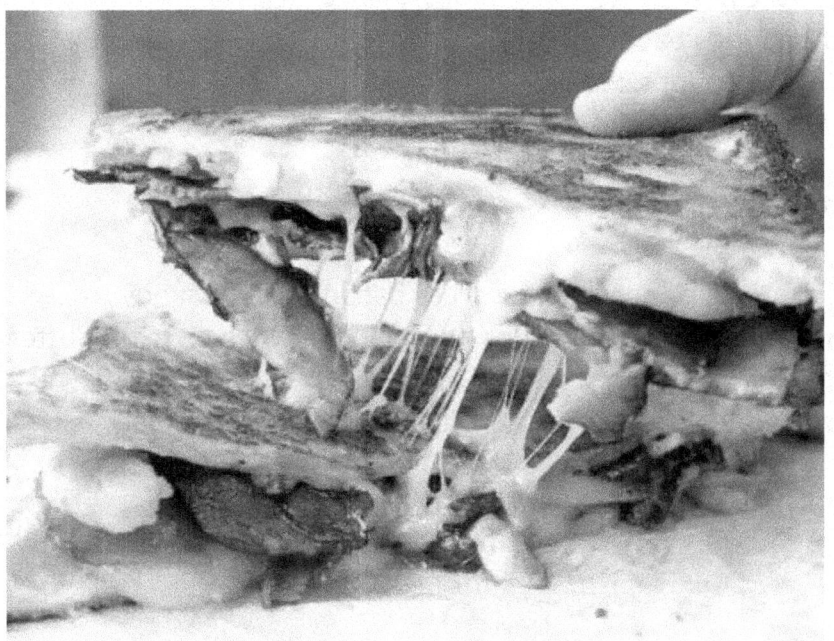

Yield: 100 Servings

INGREDIENTS:
- 12 pounds bacon; sliced
- 5 3/16 pounds cheese
- 2 pounds butter print sure
- 200 slices bread

INSTRUCTIONS
a) Fry bacon
b) Place 1 slice cheese and 2 slices bacon on each sandwich.
c) Brush lightly top and bottom of sandwiches with butter or margarine.
d) Grill until sandwiches are lightly browned on each side and cheese is melted.

99. Grilled cheese gobblers

Yield: 4 Servings

INGREDIENTS:
- 8 slices Sourdough or multigrain
- Bread
- ½ cup Cranberry sauce
- 6 ounces Turkey, cooked and sliced
- 4 ounces Cheddar cheese, mild or
- Sharp, thinly sliced
- Butter

INSTRUCTIONS

a) Spread 4 slices of bread with cranberry sauce: top with turkey, cheese and remaining bread slices.
b) Lightly spread outside of sandwiches with butter; cook in large skillet over medium-low heat until browned on both sides.

100. <u>Grilled cheese in French toast</u>

Yield: 4 Servings

INGREDIENTS:
- 2 eggs, beaten
- ¼ cup milk
- ¼ cup dry sherry
- ¼ teaspoons Worcestershire sauce
- 8 slices white bread or whole wheat bread
- 4 slices Cheddar cheese

INSTRUCTIONS

a) In a shallow bowl, combine eggs, milk, sherry and Worcestershire.

b) Assemble 4 cheese sandwiches, then dip each in the egg mixture and grill slowly in butter, turning once to get both sides golden brown.

CONCLUSION

Sandwiches are a classic and convenient meal that can be enjoyed by anyone, whether you are a busy parent, a student on-the-go, or simply looking for a tasty and satisfying meal. With the recipes shared in this article, you can create delicious sandwiches at home that are packed with flavor and sure to impress. So, next time you are in need of a quick and tasty meal, consider making a sandwich and let your taste buds be delighted.

www.ingramcontent.com/pod-product-compliance
Lightning Source LLC
Chambersburg PA
CBHW070355120526
44590CB00014B/1146